Marxism:

A Latter-day Saint Perspective

Marxism:

A Latter-day Saint Perspective

Dan Ellsworth

Eremos Books

Original Title: Marxism: A Latter-day Saint Perspective
First edition: September 13, 2024
© 2024, Dan Ellsworth
© 2024, Eremos Books
info@eremosbooks.com

Printed in the United States of America
ISBN: 979-8-9911579-0-2

In grateful memory of Alexandr Solzhenitsyn

Table of Contents

Introduction..1

Part 1: The Roots

Chapter 1: What is Marxism?..10

Part 2: The Branches (Cultural Marxism)

Chapter 2: What Did Marxism Become?................................32

Part 3: The Fruits (Neo-Marxism)

Chapter 3: Intersectionality, Identity Politics, and the Gospel.............46

Chapter 4: Critical Race Theory and the Gospel....................58

Chapter 5: Gender Theory, Queer Theory, and the Gospel..................82

Chapter 6: The Historical Fruits of Marxism........................101

Part 4: The Church and Marxism

Chapter 7: Marxism and Deconversion.................................120

Chapter 8: Marxism and Scripture...129

Chapter 9: Marxism and Satanism...145

Conclusion: Marxism and the Plans of Old...........................167

Works Cited..181

Introduction

Marxism is a term that brings nervousness and even outrage into the minds of many Latter-day Saints. On the other hand, many church members consider an aversion to Marxism to be a sign of backward thinking, a remnant of an old ideological and political battle from the 1950s that made its way into the highest levels of the church before fading into irrelevance.

Why discuss Marxism? Why rehash old controversies that only serve to divide church members?

I understand why people ask those questions, because I used to ask them. In the mid-1900s, the world was dividing into countries in alliance with the democratic West led by the United States on one hand, and countries in alliance with an undemocratic coalition of communist and communist-sympathetic states led by Russia on the other hand. For those of us who grew up during at least some of that cold war era, there are memories of constant dread around the prospect of nuclear war between the two powers. I personally remember, growing up in the 1980s, how many of our movies and books had plots based on war or spy activity between America and Russia.

And then, when the Berlin Wall fell and the Soviet Union disintegrated in 1989, the world breathed a sigh of relief. Communism was more or less vanquished, we thought, although it might continue on in some small pockets throughout the world, where a few remaining communist governments would live in denial of the collapse of their vision for the future.

Within the church, President Ezra Taft Benson had once been a politically-active apostle who thundered constant denunciations of communism, and left unsettled many members of the church who did not share his devotion to right-wing politics. But as president of the church, Ezra Taft Benson underwent a radical shift in tone, declaring in his opening press conference that "My heart has been filled with an overwhelming love and compassion for all members of the Church and our Heavenly Father's children everywhere. I love all our Father's children of every color, creed, and political persuasion. My only desire is to serve as the Lord would have me do."[1]

President Benson did not focus on communism during his ministry as president of the church. But he might have had communism in mind in a conference talk called I Testify, where he said that "A secret combination that seeks to overthrow the freedom of all lands, nations, and countries is increasing its evil influence and control over America and the entire world."[2]

Among Latter-day Saints, discussions of Marxism carry the baggage of a lot of history, whether church members are aware of that or not.

---

[1] The Ensign, "President Ezra Taft Benson Ordained Thirteenth President of the Church."

[2] Ezra Taft Benson, "I Testify"

In this book, I want to make a break from that past.

That might seem overly ambitious, but I suggest it is not, and here are three reasons why:

1. As of this writing in 2024, a large proportion of church members did not live through the cold war, so their discussions of Marxism are not dominated by the memory of 20th century conflicts over communism.

2. Since the end of the cold war, the work of Marxist academics and activists has separated Marxism from communism, whereas during the cold war era, Marxism and communism had been considered one and the same, with the terms used interchangeably. The separation of these two terms, and the recognition that they now have different meanings, invites a change in the way that we discuss them.

3. Cultural Marxism used to be dismissed as a right-wing conspiracy theory, but it has now come to fruition not just in the United States, but in other parts of the world. It is not something that is imagined; it is something we clearly observe. It can now be analyzed in very concrete terms with specific examples of how it affects individuals and societies.

Things are very different now compared to how they were in my youth, during the cold war. And that means it is time for Latter-day Saints to have a different conversation about Marxism.

Also as of this writing in 2024, there is a renewed concern over Marxism being taught and promoted in various forms in the U.S. and other parts of the world, and my mind turns to Latter-day Saint parents who are worried about their children being indoctrinated into Marxism in schools and other places. The sense of fear is very real, and I personally believe that it is a normal response to things we are observing with the spread of newer forms of Marxism, or *neo-Marxism*.

But in this book I want to equip those parents with some new understanding and new language for engaging with their children. My hope is that when a young Latter-day Saint college student gains exposure to Marxist ideas in their university studies, parents can utilize tools in this book to respond with love and confidence instead of fear. To these parents I say that if your kid in college sees some appeal in ideas promoted by Marxists, this is not an indicator that you are a failed parent, that your child is stupid or clueless, or that hope is lost. The Marxist worldview has some powerful resemblances to truths of the restored gospel, so if your child's heart and mind resonate with some of the Marxist concepts they hear in their education, I would suggest that indicates you have done well as a parent.

In conversations with people who hold a Marxist worldview, we can fully acknowledge the grains of truth in Marxism, and show how the restored gospel enables those grains to sprout into healthy and productive fruit, while Marxism turns those same grains of truth into toxic and destructive movements. This book aims to be a resource in that process of discernment and distinction.

Another motivation for my writing this book is my involvement with temple and family history work. As Latter-day Saints participating in the redemption of our ancestors who have passed on, we should expect to find among our ancestors people who participated in, and sometimes even led, Marxist movements. In the church we may even have members who are descendants of Karl Marx himself, or members of his family. I hope that this book can help church members to see their ancestors with love and understanding, rather than fear or disdain.

Finally, I also expect that as our missionary efforts proceed throughout the world, we are going to see increasing numbers of new converts who have more of a Marxist worldview than members in wealthy Western countries. I hope that these new members can be greeted with all of the warmth and care and sincere love that we offer to converts who don't have any elements of a Marxist worldview. And for church members who are not sure how to arrive to that place emotionally, I hope this book can be a resource.

This book is not meant to be an academic treatment of Marxist thinking; much of the analysis here is derived from the life and work of Karl Marx, and also some key figures who formed Marxist intellectual and political movements following his death. Along the way, I offer plenty of my own personal observations. Readers of this book will sense at several points that to study Marxism is to walk into a fight that has been going on for a long time. Students of the history of Marxism will find "classical Marxists," "open Marxists," "cultural Marxists," and more, with countless different degrees of variation between people who claim Marxism, and who deny the legitimacy of other people's claims to Marxism. Those conflicts among Marxists will never be resolved, certainly not in this book. But to understand the development of Marxism over time, we can utilize a basic working model that will resonate with Latter-day Saints: the metaphor of Marxism as a tree with roots, branches, and fruit.

The approach I am taking in this book reflects concepts taught by Jonathan Haidt, most notably in his book The

Righteous Mind.[3] There, Haidt taught that people have moral intuitions that shape our views on politics and religion. The basic idea is that conservative-leaning people feel strongly toward one set of moral intuitions and liberal/progressive people feel strongly toward the other set:

Conservative intuitions:
- Loyalty/betrayal
- Authority/subversion
- Sanctity/degradation

Liberal intuitions:
- Care/harm
- Fairness/cheating

When we engage in partisan thinking, sometimes our tendency is to speak to one set of intuitions and disregard the others. But moving through the discussion of Marxism in this book, my hope is that you, the reader, will see a discussion that is integrated, reflecting all of the intuitions in Haidt's framework. This is due to a personal theological view that I hold, that God is the perfect embodiment of all moral intuitions, not just conservative or liberal/progressive ones.

I have yet to see a book by a Latter-day Saint author that explores Marxism with attention to all of the moral intuitions, so this book is an attempt to do just that. And in the process, I expect that every reader of this book will agree with some things, and disagree with others.

At the outset, I wish to be clear about my conviction that Marxism is a worldview that has led to immense historical evil, and the branches and fruits of Marxism

---

3 Haidt, *The Righteous Mind: Why Good People Are Divided by Politics and Religion*. p.146

have become a destructive force in the present day. And yet, it is a worldview that is sometimes held by good people. Jonathan Haidt's framework of moral intuitions is useful for explaining how this is possible, and in this book I intend to speak to the moral realities that Marxism attempts to resolve. I hope that people who lean toward a Marxist worldview will see their moral concerns represented well in these pages.

My ultimate hope is that upon reading this book, Latter-day Saints will have a level of understanding that will allow them to have better conversations with loved ones and colleagues who are sympathetic to the Marxist worldview, or who may have fully embraced it.

Part 1
The Roots

Chapter 1

What is Marxism?

When we use the word Marxism, it is important to be clear as to what we are talking about. And for the purposes of this book, I am going to use a simple definition for that term: Marxism is the set of assumptions that Karl Marx held about the world in which we live.

The assumptions that Marx held about our world were extensive in their scope. Marx assumed very specific things about human nature, about society, and also about God and the nature of religion. His life's work was to make those assumptions into a set of theories that he envisioned would transform the world.

During his lifetime, Marx applied his system primarily to questions of economics, and it became called communism. Later, his system would be applied to other areas of human experience, as we will explore in the next chapter. But on a very basic level, Marx assumed some things about the world:

1. The world is divided into classes of oppressors and oppressed.

What is Marxism?

2. People working under capitalist systems are *alienated*, meaning they are not allowed to enjoy their lives and the results of their work.
3. In capitalist society there is a "base," which is the way that ordinary people and organizations live under everyday oppression. The base is created and maintained by a superstructure, which is a set of ideologies, institutions, and traditions that maintain a group's denial of access to a specific form of property (in the case of capitalism, the property is capital).

More can and will be said about the wider range of Marx's assumptions about the world, but these are the basic assumptions that form the core of his theory.[1]

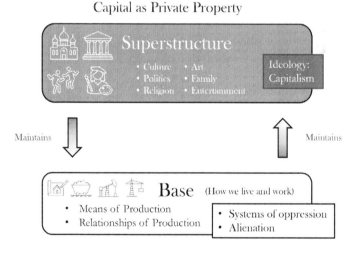

---

1 Note: I am indebted to The New Discourses for this basic model of Marxist thinking and its various applications.

In the Communist Manifesto, Marx explained that "… the theory of the Communists may be summed up in the single sentence: Abolition of private property."[2]

Marx was not claiming here that no person should ever own anything; his claim was that there is such thing as bourgeois property, property owned by the bourgeois class of people who benefit from the labor of others and maintain systems of oppression. This is an important distinction, but over time, the notion of bourgeois property as property acquired through the labor of others has become expanded among modern Marxists to include *property held due to "privilege."* We will discuss this in later chapters.

There is another assumption underlying Marxist thought and activism, and it is an extremely powerful one:

There exists an ideal society, and it is possible to achieve that ideal society without God.

This particular assumption is the heart of socialism, the idea that governments can allocate resources better than individuals in markets.

Together, these assumptions are the roots of the Marxist tree, and as we will see in the next chapter, following the time of Marx this tree trunk has sprouted sprawling branches of Marxist theories and movements that reach far beyond economic concerns.

Marxism is a Response to Unfairness

Having offered a simple definition of Marxism, we now turn to explore the nature of Marxist ideas, including

---

2   Marx, "Manifesto of the Communist Party"

What is Marxism?

what motivated Marx to develop these assumptions into a system of thought and a political movement.

Marx lived in a world that was unfair. When we think of how Marx developed his theories, we might turn to his observations about the plight of workers who were exploited by capitalist property-owners; for example, poverty-stricken farm workers living in overcrowded labor houses:

> common humanity requires that the other aspect of this evil should not be ignored .... In its higher degrees it [i.e., over-crowding] almost necessarily involves such negation of all delicacy, such unclean confusion of bodies and bodily functions, such exposure of animal and sexual nakedness, as is rather bestial than human. To be subject to these influences is a degradation which must become deeper and deeper for those on whom it continues to work. To children who are born under its curse, it must often be a very baptism into infamy. And beyond all measure hopeless is the wish that persons thus circumstanced should ever in other respects aspire to that atmosphere of civilisation which has its essence in physical and moral cleanliness.[3]

The world of Marx – 19th Century Europe – was also a world of cruel exploitation of children in child labor. Children worked long hours in dangerous conditions instead of going to school, and their work was performed in factories owned by wealthy people who sought to maximize their profits by minimizing their costs of labor. Factory owners lived comfortably compared to their workers, who usually lived in grinding poverty.

---

3   Dr. Julian Hunter, quoted in Marx, *Economic Manuscripts: Capital Vol. I - Chapter One*.

The pain of the common workers was not just noticed by radical intellectuals like Karl Marx. Observing the plight of workers, Brigham Young commented that "The course pursued by men of business in the world has a tendency to make a few rich, and to sink the masses of the people in poverty and degradation."[4]

It might be hard for modern, prosperous Latter-day Saints in the West to imagine why Brigham Young would say something like this, but Brigham Young and a number of other early church leaders knew the experience of poverty. They also knew firsthand the pain of being exploited by bankers and property owners. Many of the early converts to the church came from Europe, leaving situations of severe exploitation. When Brigham Young spoke to these realities, it likely resonated deeply within them. In another context, Brigham said to the saints:

> Shall I give you my ideas in brief with regard to business and business transactions? Here for instance, a merchant comes to our neighborhood with a stock of goods; he sells them at from two to ten hundred per cent above what they cost. As a matter of course he soon becomes wealthy, and after a time he will be called a millionaire, when perhaps he was not worth a dollar when he commenced to trade. You will hear many say of such person, what a nice man he is, and what a great financier he is! My feeling of such a man is, he is a great cheat, a deceiver, a liar! He imposes on the people, he takes that which does not belong to him, and is a living monument of falsehood.
>
> ...the great majority of men who have amassed great

---

4 Young and Widstoe, *Discourses of Brigham Young*. p.454

wealth have done it at the expense of their fellows.[5]

These are only some examples of the warnings and condemnations he spoke surrounding exploitative business practices, and it is important to be familiar with these teachings as they show that commentators like Marx were not alone in their understanding that capitalist societies were sometimes characterized by real and painful oppression.

It is also important to stress here that these remarks from Brigham Young, and other similar remarks from church leaders, do not in any way reflect a Marxist vision of the world. No prophet in this dispensation has ever taught against the ownership of private property, and they have never shared the central Marxist premise that there exists an ideal society that can be created apart from God.

Marxism Stems From Marx's Personal Life

One of the most influential German thinkers during the time of Marx was Friederich Nietzsche, and in Nietzsche's writings Beyond Good and Evil, he made the following statements:

> The greater part of the conscious thinking of a philosopher is secretly influenced by his instincts, and forced into definite channels…
>
> It has gradually become clear to me what every great philosophy up till now has consisted of—namely, the confession of its originator, and a species of involuntary and unconscious auto-biography…
>
> In the philosopher…there is absolutely nothing impersonal; and above all, his morality furnishes a

---

5   Young and Widstoe, *Discourses* p. 457

> decided and decisive testimony as to WHO HE IS,— that is to say, in what order the deepest impulses of his nature stand to each other…[6]

What Nietzsche observed of philosophers is true of all thinkers, including Marx. When people offer grand explanations of how the world works, what truth is, how human beings function, what is the ideal society, and so forth, it is impossible to do that without painting portraits of themselves. In our commentary about the world, we show others what we love, desire, fear, and hate. We reveal our life experiences and how we have responded to them. We also reveal our lack of life experiences, and how our lack of experience leaves us with gaps in our understanding.

When we talk about the creation of Marxism, it is important to do as Nietzsche suggested and examine some personal dimensions of the life of Karl Marx. As Marx biographer Robert Payne expressed,

> Out of the squalor and misery of his life came those insistent fantasies of power, and we shall not understand Marx unless we realize how deeply and pervasively his strange and unhappy life was reflected in his dreams. He announced his doctrines and theories as the result of impersonal scholarship. In fact they derived as much from his private fantasies as from the revolutionary traditions of his time.[7]

To understand Marx's ideas and impulses, we need to understand the basic contours of his personal story.

Karl Marx was born in 1818 to a Jewish family that converted to Christianity in Germany in order to avoid the

---

6   Nietzsche, *Beyond Good and Evil*.

7   Payne, *Marx*. p.12

What is Marxism?

exclusion of antisemitism. As Karl grew into adolescence he behaved like any normal Christian youth of his time, but when he left home in 1835 to begin studies at Bonn University, he ran wild with drinking, partying, and spending money far beyond his means. During that time, Karl joined a poetry club, which continued one of his favorite hobbies. He also began associating with other people who considered themselves "revolutionaries," advocating for radical transformation of society.

In the summer of 1836, Karl returned home to Trier and got secretly engaged to Jenny Von Westphalen, the daughter of one of his mentors.

Following that summer, Karl moved to pursue studies at the University of Berlin. Upon arriving there, Karl isolated himself from others and became consumed in his studies, while also writing letters and poems to his fiancé Jenny. In March 1837, Karl's father Heinrich Marx wrote him a letter expressing worry over his son's behavior and his life trajectory. Karl's father wrote with concern,

> My heart sometimes delights in thoughts of you and your future. And yet sometimes I can't resist sad, foreboding, frightening ideas when the thought hits me like lightning: does a heart match your head, your disposition? — Does it have room for the earthly but tender sentiments which, in this vale of tears, are such essential consolation to a sensitive soul? Since it is evidently animated and ruled by a demon not bestowed on all men, is this demon of a heavenly or of a Faustian nature? Will you — and this is not the least tormenting doubt for my heart — ever be receptive to truly human domestic happiness? ... will you ever be able to spread happiness to those closest to you?[8]

[8] Marx and Engels, *Collected Works, Vol 1*

This reference to a "demon" shows that Heinrich Marx perceived an unusually intense driving force in his son. Karl had abandoned the study of law and was now devouring lots of different books of politics, history, and other kinds of information. His personal behavior was manifesting an alarming lack of self-control.

Recall Heinrich Marx's concern that the "demon" driving Marx might have been "Faustian"- this was a reference to Goethe's play Faust, where the main character makes a life-consuming deal with a devil named Mephistopheles. Heinrich's reference to Faust was perhaps more perceptive than he knew, because Karl Marx had become powerfully influenced by that play and especially the demonic character of Mephistopheles.

In one of his writings, Marx quoted a simple statement from Mephistopheles: "All that exists deserves to perish."[9] This might sound like an extreme statement, not reflecting Marx's personal views, except for the fact that so much of his personal poetry contained fantasies of both personal annihilation and world-destruction.

Marx has long been regarded as an atheist, but his poetry reveals that his worldview was not atheistic; it was *misotheistic*. In contrast with atheism, which is a lack of belief in God, Misotheism is *a personal hatred of God*. Karl's poem called Human Pride, written to his fiancé Jenny, contains the following verses:

> *And it wavers not a whit*
> *Where the very God-Thought fares,*
> *On its breast will cherish it;*
> *Soul's own greatness is its lofty Prayer.*
> *Soul its greatness must devour,*

---

9   Marx, "18th Brumaire of Louis Bonaparte. Karl Marx 1852."

What is Marxism?

> *In its greatness must go down;*
> *Then volcanoes seethe and roar,*
> *   And lamenting Demons gather round.*
> *Soul, succumbing haughtily,*
> *   Raises up a throne to giant derision;*
> *Downfall turns to Victory,*
> *   Hero's prize is proud renunciation.*
> *Then the gauntlet do I fling*
> *   Scornful in the World's wide open face.*
> *Down the giant She-Dwarf, whimpering,*
> *Plunges, cannot crush my happiness.*
> *Like unto a God I dare*
> *   Through that ruined realm in triumph roam.*
> *Every word is Deed and Fire,*
> *   And my bosom like the Maker's own.*[10]

This poem expresses defiance and personal loathing toward God, whom Karl ridicules as a "giant she-dwarf." Karl expresses a similar misotheism in his poem Invocation of One in Despair:

> *So a god has snatched from me my all*
> *In the curse and rack of Destiny.*
> *All his worlds are gone beyond recall!*
> *Nothing but revenge is left to me!*
> *On myself revenge I'll proudly wreak,*
> *On that being, that enthroned Lord,*
> *Make my strength a patchwork of what's weak,*
> *Leave my better self without reward!*
> *I shall build my throne high overhead,*
> *Cold, tremendous shall its summit be.*
> *For its bulwark-- superstitious dread,*
> *For its Marshall--blackest agony.*
> *Who looks on it with a healthy eye,*
> *Shall turn back, struck deathly pale and dumb;*

---

10 Marx, "Human Pride"

> *Clutched by blind and chill Mortality*
> *May his happiness prepare its tomb.*
> *And the Almighty's lightning shall rebound*
> *From that massive iron giant.*
> *If he bring my walls and towers down,*
> *Eternity shall raise them up, defiant.*[11]

In this poem we note the phrase "Who looks on it with a healthy eye...," and the notion of a healthy eye comes from the teaching of Jesus in Matthew 6:22, "If your eye is healthy, your whole body will be filled with light." Marx suggests here that someone in the healthy spiritual state described by Jesus, would be horrified at the realm Marx is imagining to create.

These misotheistic poems show that at some point in his university years, Karl had gone from an awareness of Christian understanding of God, to something very different. And his poetry shows a heart overflowing with evil. Robert Payne summarizes, "If we isolate the images [Marx] employs in his works, the images which constantly recur and which he uses with ferocious effect, we find that they are nearly always concerned with mutilation or death, torture, ruptured wombs, the executioner advancing out of the darkness with leisurely tread. His mind moved at ease among images of corruption and damnation, of sudden sprawling deaths and agonies."[12]

During his time at the University of Berlin, Karl devoured the writings of Georg Hegel, a philosopher who taught that truth is arrived at through a process of bringing an idea into destructive conflict with its opposite, and then allowing that destruction to give rise to a better idea.

---

11 Marx, "Invocation of one in despair"

12 Payne, *Marx*. P. 317

What is Marxism?

For a number of students at Berlin University, Hegel's ideas transformed their entire view of reality. This was the case with Karl Marx, who joined a social group known as the Young Hegelians. Among that group were radical thinkers who would have a powerful impact on Karl Marx. Much of his thinking around alienation, criticism, consciousness, religion, and other concepts can be traced to his activities among the Young Hegelians.

When we discuss people who had a significant impact upon Karl Marx, a pattern emerges. We can observe his close contact with people and we can observe how their thinking shaped his own thinking. We can even observe him borrowing other people's exact language in his own writings. But there is almost always an awful breakup, a falling out. Throughout his life Karl Marx ended up in sharp conflict with his associates, an exception being his longtime collaborator Friederich Engels.

One of Karl's initial mentors among the Young Hegelians was Bruno Bauer, a philosopher who had been a prominent student of Hegel. Consider Karl Marx's famous claim that "religion is the opium of the people" in light of Bruno Bauer's statement that "...in the true Christian state theology…can, through influence similar to that of opium create a situation in which not a spark of opposition can be found and all human tendencies slumber"[13]

Marx's pattern was essentially Hegelian; he took ideas of people around him, then attacked those ideas and their authors, and developed what he claimed to be his own correct understanding of the underlying concept.

---

13 Rosen, "The Influence of Bruno Bauer on Marx' Concept Of Alienation."

Bruno Bauer's younger brother Edgar was also among the Young Hegelians, and he wrote a poem of Karl Marx:

> *Who is in pursuit with wild impetuousness?*
> *A dark fellow from Trier, a remarkable monster.*
> *Neither walks nor hops, but springs upon his heels*
> *And rages with anger and as if he wants to grab*
> *The wide skies and drag them to earth,*
> *stretches his arms wide out to the heavens.*
> *With clenched, angry fists, he rages interminably,*
> *As if ten thousand devils had him by the hair.*[14]

Marx's contentious personality contributed to the implosion of the Young Hegelians, and after he started a political journal, it stopped after publishing just one issue.

Following Marx's marriage, he and Jenny moved to Paris, and not long after, he met his lifelong friend, Friederich Engels. He also began collaborating with anarchist revolutionary Mikhail Bakunin, who wrote of Satan in the garden of Eden,

> But here steps in Satan, the eternal rebel, the first freethinker and the emancipator of worlds. He makes man ashamed of his bestial ignorance and obedience; he emancipates him, stamps upon his brow the seal of liberty and humanity, in urging him to disobey and eat of the fruit of knowledge.[15]

Bakunin's reimagining of Satan as a noble and defiant figure was a view commonly held among revolutionary thinkers around Marx, and the misotheism in Marx's writings indicates that he shared their view that defiance of God is something to aspire to, something worth

---

14 Demunsereeuw, *Deconstructing Karl Marx & Communism: Character Study & Metaphysical Analysis of Communism*. p.41

15 Bakunin, "God and the State - Chapter I."

What is Marxism?

celebrating. Before Marx's move to Paris, the Young Hegelians had impacted his thinking to a great degree, and some of them offered sharp criticisms of Christianity. In a view Marx would come to embrace, they viewed Christianity as having created mental passivity among the working class. As Marx's mentor Bruno Bauer wrote, "Faith, the accomplished spiritual human sacrifice, is passivity, suffering, and unfreedom raised to a state, to the law of man."[16] Bauer and others in Marx's circle had viewed religious Christian faith as the mechanism that maintained the status quo in society. Bauer said of the Christian narrative of Jesus,

> On earth [Jesus] would be a thousand times more necessary and useful to man than in heaven, if what we say about him in good Jewish fashion is true, that God will give him the kingdoms of the world and through him restore peace to the whole earth. What reasonable reason can Christians give as to why God did not keep his word to the Lord Jesus? Why did he take him to heaven if he is to be a Lord on earth and to judge the dead and the living in the way we imagine? Why must the devil whom he is supposed to have overcome, still rule the whole world more than 1700 years after his overcoming and leave the conqueror behind? Why did he (the Lord Jesus) not take the kingdom immediately after his resurrection, as his Father had promised him? What was the reason that he had to ascend to heaven and in the meantime let everything on earth go topsy-turvy.[17]

---

16 Bauer, *Das Entdeckte Christentum: Eine Erinnerung an Das Neunzehnte Jahrhundert*. p.96

17 Ibid., p.101

In contrast with this picture of Jesus as an ineffective savior, Marx's circle of associates had viewed Satan as the honest disruptor who opened humanity's eyes to reality and brought them to consciousness. In their eyes, Satan was the hero of the biblical story.

It is interesting to recall that when Karl Marx had been studying at the University of Berlin, there was a period of three years where he took only two courses, and one of those was a course on the book of Isaiah taught by his antisemitic and anti-Christian mentor Bruno Bauer. The book of Isaiah contains the most vivid Old Testament prophecy of Christ (in chapter 53) and also the most vivid Old Testament description of the fall of Satan during our premortal existence (in chapter 14). In the King James translation of the latter passages, we read:

> *How art thou fallen from heaven, O Lucifer, son of the morning! how art thou cut down to the ground, which didst weaken the nations!*
>
> *For thou hast said in thine heart, I will ascend into heaven, I will exalt my throne above the stars of God: I will sit also upon the mount of the congregation, in the sides of the north:*
>
> *I will ascend above the heights of the clouds; I will be like the most High.*
>
> *Yet thou shalt be brought down to hell, to the sides of the pit. (Isaiah 14:12-13)*

This language in Isaiah 14 describing the fall of Satan is couched within a diatribe against the king of Babylon, suggesting an archetypal pattern shared between the two. And in the poetry of Marx, we see him assuming this archetype for himself:

What is Marxism?

Isaiah	Marx
For thou hast said in thine heart, I will ascend into heaven, **I will exalt my throne above** the stars of God…	**I shall build my throne high overhead**, Cold, tremendous shall its summit be[18]
I will ascend above the heights of the clouds; **I will be like the most High**	**Like unto a God** I dare… Every word is Deed and Fire, And **my bosom like the Maker's own**[19]
Yet thou shalt be **brought down to hell**	Thus Heaven I've forfeited, I know it full well. My soul, once true to God, Is **chosen for Hell**.[20]

It is hard to say definitively whether the admiring of the Satan figure in the Old Testament was something that Karl Marx learned from his revolutionary colleagues, or whether he brought it to their conversations as a perspective he had acquired on his own. But it is clear that Satan-admiration was a shared element of the revolutionary worldview held by Marx and his colleagues.

For much of his life Marx was a miserable person, and he imposed severe hardships on his family. He prioritized his hobbies over making a living, so throughout most of his years he was constantly asking for money from his parents and friends. Due to his constant revolutionary activities, Marx was eventually expelled from France and moved his family to Belgium, was expelled from Belgium and moved back to France, was expelled from France again, and moved back to Prussia before being expelled from Prussia and finally settling in London, where he would remain for the rest of his life.

---

18   Marx, "Invocation of One in Despair."

19   Marx, "Human Pride."

20   Marx, "The Pale Maiden."

His family life was unstable, and his marriage was volatile like his personality. Biographer Robert Payne writes,

> That Marx should have spent so much of his life in a helpless rage against the world is less surprising than the fact that he seemed unaware that he was driven by it, and made no effort to moderate it. In letter after letter he roars his disgust at the world and at people, with unbridled malevolence, drawing on the resources of gutter language in order to emphasize his passionate rejection. Friends of many years suddenly become enemies of the moment, and he exhausts the vocabulary of vituperation in denouncing them.[21]

Eventually, Marx gained a long-term source of income through a family inheritance, which led him to live comfortably for the last 15 years of his life. In 1864, Marx joined the International Workingmen's Association, sometimes called simply the International. This was a group of workers who were looking to promote socialism in Europe, and Marx maneuvered his way into leadership in the organization.

Within the International, Marx engaged in a fierce power struggle with his long associate Mikhail Bakunin. He structured the leadership of the organization in a way that consolidated his authority, and his feud with Bakunin culminated in Marx's effort to move the International to America, destroying the organization in the process. Following this ordeal, Bakunin's health began to fail and he reminisced of Marx: "Marx does not believe in God, but he believes much in himself, and makes everyone subservient

---

21 Payne, *Marx*. p.316

What is Marxism?

to himself. His heart is not full of love, but of gall, and he has very little sympathy for the human race."[22]

This glimpse of the life of Marx is important because, as we will see, elements of his tormented life are reflected in the lives of many world leaders and influential theorists who adopted Marx's worldview. The political is always personal. It is not possible to separate the original roots and trunk of Marxism from its later branches and fruits, which we will begin to explore in the next chapter.

Some Points of Reflection

Marx's impact on humanity would end up being vast, but only after his death. His impact on the people around him can be seen in the fact that only 11 people attended his funeral. By the time of his death, his caustic personality and terrible behavior had driven away almost all of his friends and the numerous people who had once admired him.

We began this chapter with the claim that the worldview that Karl Marx developed and shaped into a movement, was a response to pain. The world around Karl Marx was profoundly unfair, and this was the painful reality for most of humanity in the time of Marx. But Marx's personal life modeled a set of responses to pain- the pain of loss of loved ones; the pain of exclusion; the pain of confusion; the pain of striving to make ends meet financially; the pain of failure; the pains of rejection; loneliness; and more. These pains are all normal parts of the human experience, and Karl Marx knew them on a personal level.

---

22 Ibid., p.451

Christianity offers a particular set of responses to life's pain: it offers clear identity in God and Christ; perspective about life's difficulties; a sense of purpose and meaning; a healthy and supportive community with soul-strengthening opportunities for human connection; and personal communion with God.

When Marx rejected Christianity in his formative young adult years, he joined other communities where people's responses to personal pain were very different from those of traditional Christians. Without a sense of meaning in life, people and societies tend to respond to pain with denial, numbing, avoidance, violence, grasping for control, and any number of other coping strategies. Beginning with the spending and drinking and other behaviors of his university years, we see those coping strategies employed constantly throughout the life of Karl Marx.

We mentioned earlier the influence of Georg Hegel, and how his ideas powerfully influenced the generation of Marx. When Hegel suggested that progress is found in bringing opposition to a thing in order to arrive at a better version of that thing, I doubt if he and the people who adopted his basic notion of progress understood how it would be applied by so many people as a way of responding to even the basic discomforts of life. Marx and others seem to have adopted this Hegelian mechanism in twisted ways, as their basic mode of engagement toward other people and toward society: see a person or institution and whatever they have of value (like ideas or roles), then criticize, subvert, humiliate, co-opt, and steal.

In modern psychology there are categories of what are called *personality disorders*, such as oppositional defiant disorder and the "Cluster B" of antisocial

What is Marxism?

personality disorder, borderline personality disorder, histrionic personality disorder, and narcissistic personality disorder. Surveying the life of Karl Marx, it is clear that his "crowd," his revolutionary circles, were snake pits of entitlement, deception, and vitriol. It is hard to say whether revolutionary ideologies attracted people with personality disorders, or whether personality disorders developed and proliferated in response to people's embrace of revolutionary ideologies.

Regardless, it is clear that the Marxist worldview emerged from that toxic stew, as a maladaptive and delusional response to pain both in society and in the personal life of Karl Marx.

Part 2: The Branches
Cultural Marxism

Chapter 2

What Did Marxism Become?

The influence of Marx began to spread late in his life, but its spread was very slow. Historian David McLellan explains that "Marx's views made such slow progress initially that it has been calculated that by 1880 there were only five men in Germany who had a well-founded understanding of his economics."[1] Eventually, though, Marxism became the basis for revolutionary movements in places like Russia, China, and South America. We will explore those in more detail in a later chapter, but for now, suffice it to say that the political movements that emerged from Marxism turned out to be oppressive failures.

This reality caused deep dissonance and frustration among people who had believed that the Marxist worldview was essentially correct. What went wrong? How could it be that the masses of the working class throughout the world were not awakened to their own alienation, and their suffering under systems of oppression? What could

---

1   David McLellan, *Marxism After Marx*, p.23

What Did Marxism Become?

possibly be the reason that so many people in capitalist societies tended to report high levels of life satisfaction?

These kinds of questions among Marxist activists led to the sprouting of new branches of Marxist thinking that attempted to explain these ironies that were so frustrating in the minds of Marxists. Here we can offer a basic survey of some of the major events and figures who formed the modern branches of Marxism that took shape after the death of Karl Marx.

Following the death of Karl Marx in 1883, there arose some scattered efforts among socialist groups in Europe to form a new iteration of the International, the activist organization that Marx had taken over and destroyed in his later years.

In 1889, the Second International held its first meeting, and the organization was full of factional conflict until it broke apart with the beginning of the first world war. But notably, Russian revolutionary Vladimir Lenin was a member of the second International from 1905, and his own interpretation of Marxism was being formed during that time through his study of Marx's writings and through his association with Marxist revolutionaries.

Vladimir Lenin's approach to revolution in Russia had a profound impact on an Italian activist named Antonio Gramsci, who sprouted a very important branch of Marxist thinking. Lenin adapted Marxism and argued that the socialist utopia envisioned in Marxist thinking could not be achieved until intellectuals had fully indoctrinated the working classes and awakened their class consciousness. Lenin saw intellectuals as central in the goals of the revolution, whereas before, much of Marxist thinking assumed that the working class itself would be the source of the new consciousness that would bring the revolution.

Antonio Gramsci was a Marxist activist in Italy who agreed with Lenin about the role of intellectuals. Gramsci developed a notion of cultural hegemony, claiming that institutions of culture – churches, educational organizations, and more – exercise a form of mind-control over the public, keeping them from awakening to their class consciousness.

Recall that in Marxist thinking there is a base of the common people's lived oppression, and above that base there is a superstructure of society that creates and maintains the systems of people's oppression. Rather than focus on base or superstructure, Gramsci treated them more like a single system. He insisted that when the elites in society – the bourgeois – exercise cultural hegemony, they actually make the working class of people desire their own oppression because they have been conditioned to desire it. The systems of oppression in society come to be understood by everyone as common sense, obvious, just the way things are.

Gramsci thought that the solution to this problem of cultural hegemony should be the infiltration of the institutions that create culture, in order to reshape their purposes in service of the revolution. When a society's institutions are shaped by intellectuals in the direction of progress, the new hegemony can reshape society toward the fulfillment of Marx's vision. Gramsci was a major figure in the branching of Marxism after Marx to different areas of focus on culture, and this trend became known as *cultural Marxism*.

The various branches of cultural Marxism developed into a variety of movements that we now refer to as *neo-Marxism*, and we will explore those in later chapters.

The Frankfurt School

The Frankfurt School is another name for an organization called the Institute for Social Research. It was founded in Frankfurt, Germany in 1923, and later in 1930, Max Horkheimer took over the institute as its director. The institute then moved to the United States in 1936, returning to Germany after World War II. The Frankfurt School became the center of cultural Marxism studies, and sparked new branches of Marxist thinking that began to sprout in the mid-1900s and grew into the powerful neo-Marxist movements that have become so influential in the present-day in the United States and Europe.

Max Horkheimer and **Theodore Adorno** were two of the primary figures in establishing the basic approach and assumptions of the Frankfurt School. They shared the Marxist perspective of Antonio Gramsci, that the reason for the failure of Marxist movements to achieve Marx's vision throughout the world had to do with the power of the superstructure in keeping the working classes incapable of seeing their own oppression. In a video interview, Horkheimer explained that their Marxist approach was a continuation of Marxist thinking, but also an adaptation of Marxist theory:

> This sociology [of the Frankfurt School] went beyond the critical theory of society conceived by Marx in order to reflect reality more adequately. One point is very important. For Marx had an ideal of a society of free human beings. He believed that this capitalist society would necessarily have to be overcome by the solidarity spelled by the increasing immiseration of the working class. This idea is wrong. This society in which we live does not immiserate the workers but helps them to build a better life. And apart from that, Marx did not see that

freedom and justice are dialectical concepts. The more freedom, the less justice and the more justice, the less freedom. The critical theory which I conceived later is based on the idea that one cannot determine, what is good, what a good, a free society would look like from within the society which we live in. We lack the means. But in our work we can bring up the negative aspects of this society, which we want to change.[2]

Horkheimer was instrumental in promoting *critical theory*, the use of academic theories in the service of activism. This is different from the normal academic ideal of theory, which is that theory should provide explanations for reality. Ideally, a researcher sees data and develops theories to explain those data. The theory is not tainted by biases or by personal agenda, because those are things that can compromise our ability to perceive what is true. The academic ideal is for a researcher to be neutral in their search for the truth.

But in the Frankfurt School, Marxist academics rejected the idea that academic research should be neutral, because they claimed it *cannot* be neutral, and even if it could be, neutrality would not be an ideal because it would not actively move society in a particular Marxist direction. Max Horkheimer explicitly said of critical theory:

> The concepts which emerge under its influence are critical of the present. The Marxist categories of class, exploitation, surplus value, profit, pauperization, and breakdown are elements in a conceptual whole, and the meaning of this whole is to be sought not in the preservation of contemporary society but in its

[2] YouTube, "Max Horkheimer on Critical Theory".

transformation into the right kind of society.[3]

In their focus on transformation of the superstructure of society — the cultural factors that they believed were keeping society from awakening to new consciousness — Horkheimer and Adorno taught a concept called *the culture industry*. Similar to Gramsci, they saw capitalist institutions like the entertainment industry shaping people's tastes and desires in ways that shut down any instincts that people might have to resist or to dissent.

Horkheimer and Adorno were intensely critical toward the enlightenment, the historical movement away from religion and tradition toward science and rationality. They maintained that the enlightenment failed to live up to its promises, and that enlightenment thinking was used to develop authoritarianism, antisemitism, and a number of other irrational, oppressive systems.

Herbert Marcuse was another prominent Marxist member of the Frankfurt School, and he is famous for teaching the idea of *repressive tolerance*. In Marcuse's view, tolerance was a corrupted value in free societies because tolerance allowed for the expression of ideas that he considered to be oppressive and damaging. Marcuse argued that in order for tolerance to be beneficial, it should be partisan- that is, tolerance should be aimed at achieving the objectives of a specific group of people who understand what is best for society:

> …this tolerance cannot be indiscriminate and equal with respect to the contents of expression, neither in word nor in deed; it cannot protect false words and wrong deeds which demonstrate that they contradict

[3] Horkheimer, "Traditional and Critical Theory," *Critical Theory: Selected Essays*. p. 218

> and counteract the' possibilities of liberation. Such indiscriminate tolerance is justified in harmless debates, in conversation, in academic discussion; it is indispensable in the scientific enterprise, in private religion. But society cannot be indiscriminate where the pacification of existence, where freedom and happiness themselves are at stake: here, certain things cannot be said, certain ideas cannot be expressed, certain policies cannot be proposed, certain behavior cannot be permitted without making tolerance an instrument for the continuation of servitude.[4]

Marcuse saw tolerance as being a virtue only when it could be employed to allow the expression of a specific viewpoint, and the viewpoint of Marcuse was a Marxist viewpoint.

Erich Fromm was a Marxist psychologist who joined the Frankfurt school in 1930, and developed a theory to explain people's tendencies to willingly surrender our autonomy to other people and institutions.

Fromm diverged from the thinking of some other members of the Frankfurt School, who acknowledged that Marx had been wrong about various elements of his theories. Instead, Fromm was very emphatic in his insistence that Marx was correct but misunderstood, not only by his critics in Western capitalist countries but also by the Marxist movement that led to the establishment of the Soviet Union.

Fromm had been raised in a very religious Jewish family, and he acknowledged that Marx's system of thought was essentially religious in nature:

> Does not all this mean that Marx's socialism is the

---

4   Marcuse, "Repressive Tolerance."

realization of the deepest religious impulses common to the great humanistic religions of the past? Indeed it does, provided we understand that Marx, like Hegel and like many others, expresses his concern for man's soul, not in theistic, but in philosophical language.[5]

Erich Fromm shared another thing in common with most of the Frankfurt school: with the exception of Herbert Marcuse, they stopped seeing themselves as revolutionaries, and like Marx, they adopted "bourgeois," upper-class, comfortable lifestyles as they developed and promoted their theories.

Eventually Erich Fromm left the Frankfurt School, to a great degree over disputes with other scholars there. In particular, Fromm had started a project to research whether specific personality traits lead to embrace of authoritarianism, and his research pointed to a conclusion that other Frankfurt School scholars found upsetting: authoritarian tendencies are not only found on the political right, but also the left. Later, Theodore Adorno and another team of researchers would publish *The Authoritarian Personality*, a study that contradicted Fromm and painted a picture of authoritarianism being an entirely right-wing phenomenon.

Beyond the Frankfurt School

Michel Foucault was born in 1926 in France, and studied under several prominent Marxist theorists in his university studies. At one point he joined the French communist party, but he never embraced Marxist theory to a degree that would make him a long-term proponent of

---

5   Kamau-Mitchell, "On Erich Fromm: Why He Left the Frankfurt School."

Marxism in the commonly-understood sense of defending Marx and his theories to the world. However, his approach to philosophy ended up being very much aligned with the purposes of the Frankfurt School, and we include him here because Foucault's ideas have been grafted onto all major branches of modern neo-Marxist thinking. Despite his skepticism about elements of Marxist theory, Foucault's thinking has become an important element of branches of neo-Marxist theory in the present day.

The thinking of Michel Foucault was centered on questions of power, and one of his most well-known ideas is that all of human discourse is oriented toward the structuring of power. Foucault also leveled strong criticisms at the fields of psychiatry and criminal justice, and he is considered by many to be a major voice in the intellectual movement called postmodernism.

The Combahee River Collective was a group of black lesbian feminist activists in Boston in the 1970s, who formed into a group based on Marxist collectivist ideas. They produced an influential statement that reads in part as follows:

> Although we are in essential agreement with Marx's theory as it applied to the very specific economic relationships he analyzed, we know that his analysis must be extended further in order for us to understand our specific economic situation as Black women.[6]

Here the Combahee River Collective explains that their approach is essentially Marxist, but echoing the understanding of Gramsci and the Frankfurt School, these activists understood that the problem with Marxism is that it was applied too narrowly to economic theory and

---

6   "The Combahee River Collective Statement."

needed to be "extended further." Their statement views economic oppression as only one form of oppression that they were experiencing; they viewed themselves as "actively committed to struggling against racial, sexual, heterosexual, and class oppression, and see as our particular task the development of integrated analysis and practice based upon the fact that the major systems of oppression are interlocking."[7]

The Combahee River Collective's statement also introduced the concept of identity politics:

> This focusing upon our own oppression is embodied in the concept of identity politics. We believe that the most profound and potentially most radical politics come directly out of our own identity, as opposed to working to end somebody else's oppression.[8]

Whereas traditional political movements had been oriented around building consensus to create a movement that could acquire and exercise political power, identity politics was narrowly focused on advocating for the interests and the power-aspirations of a particular identity group.

Derrick Bell was a legal scholar who was instrumental in the development of critical race theory, which takes the Marxist template of systems of oppression in a superstructure, and applies that template to race-based forms of oppression. Bell was a major influence on Kimberlé Crenshaw and many other scholars who have developed the academic and activist dimensions of critical race theory.

---

7   Ibid.

8   Ibid.

Kimberlé Crenshaw is a law professor at Columbia University who in 1989 coined the term *intersectionality*, which further develops the notion of layers of oppression that had been described by the Combahee River Collective. Intersectionality is sometimes seen as critical of Marxism, but this is true only in the same sense that was offered by the Combahee River collective, who maintained that Marxism was too narrowly focused on one form of oppression (economic), and a person's experience of oppression can sometimes have more than one dimension, all of which must be explored together. Intersectionality does not reject Marxism; it just seeks to enlarge the scope of Marxist concerns.

Similar to Michel Foucault's notions of discourse and power, Crenshaw's explanation of intersectionality has become a core element of the modern Marxist toolset, and has helped to achieve the aims of the Frankfurt School and the Combahee River Collective in expanding the application of the Marxist worldview to more areas of human experience.

Judith Butler and **Gayle Rubin** are two of the primary figures in the development of gender theory and queer theory, which have become close and intertwined branches of modern neo-Marxist thinking. Butler's most prominent claim is that gender is not tied to any objective reality, such as biological sex. Rather, gender is socially constructed; it is something we develop out of our culture and other factors. And gender is something we *perform*, rather than being an objective reality of our lives.

Gayle Rubin's writings have more to do with the nature of sexual attractions and desires. Rubin applies a Marxist view to people's judgments around what is good or natural sexuality, arguing that norms and ideals in sexuality are a form of oppression. It follows that when institutions in the domains of religion and science express clear principles around what is normal or ideal, they are contributing to the oppressive superstructure of society.

Summary- The Branching of a Worldview

These are some of the main figures who have sprouted and grown the branches of Marxism beyond its initial focus on economics, and extended the Marxist worldview to the realms of culture and politics.

In the chapters that follow, we will move from our discussion of the modern branches of Marxism to a closer examination of its activist fruits — what we sometimes call neo-Marxism — and the observable impacts of neo-Marxism upon individuals and groups and nations. As we proceed, we will also examine examples of ways that the Marxist worldview aims to achieve righteous and worthy objectives, but falls short of what is possible to experience in the gospel of Jesus Christ.

A common thread in these discussions has to do with how we respond to reality. In his book *The Road Less Traveled*, M. Scott Peck taught that

> Truth or reality is avoided when it is painful. We can revise our maps only when we have the discipline to overcome that pain. To have such discipline, we must be totally dedicated to truth. That is to say that we must always hold truth, as best we can determine it, to be more important, more vital to our self-interest, than our comfort.[9]

---

9   Peck, *The Road Less Travelled: A New Psychology of Love, Traditional Values and Spiritual Growth*. p.50

Beginning with Marx, we see currents of unreality and delusion that flow through the Marxist worldview. Some of the strongest delusions in Marxism have to do with human nature; we see a basic Marxist refusal to understand how people work, how human beings respond to incentives. When we glimpse some of the more painful realities of human behavior, it can be overwhelming, and this is especially true when we are not developing God's perspective of reality.

God abides all of reality perfectly, even all of the most horrible and unfair things that happen in our world. Growth and development in the gospel is in part a matter of allowing God to facilitate shifts in our souls that move us toward God's view of reality, and toward God's perfect responses to reality.

In Marxism we see people's attempts to respond to reality after they have removed God from the equation. Instead of allowing God to endow us with the capacity to live well in reality – even difficult and painful reality – we see in Marxism a different response to reality: a turn toward *theory*, an intellectual realm where people can pretend that reality is something other than what it is.

The fruits of this turn toward theory instead of God are going to be difficult to discuss in the coming chapters, but the discussion is important as it brings clarity to our choices and those of people we love.

Part 3: The Fruits
neo-Marxism

Chapter 3

Intersectionality, Identity Politics, and the Gospel

We begin our discussion of the fruits of Marxism with a discussion of intersectionality, and we do this for a reason: intersectionality is perhaps the core animating idea that flows through the minds of modern neo-Marxist thinkers and activists. When we understand the appeal of intersectionality and how it plays out in real human experience, it becomes possible to make sense of Marxist behavior that we see in many different environments, especially in universities and on social media.

Recall that intersectionality is the idea that different kinds of oppression can be experienced at the same time. These experiences of oppression can overlap, and together they can create unique new forms and magnitudes of oppression. So intersectional theory says that in order to make society more fair, we need to examine how different kinds of oppression function together, and then address the unique challenges that result.

On a very basic level, this is factually true. If I am living in a society where maleness and light complexion are the norm, then as a white male, I am unlikely to know the social exclusion and sometimes the fear and avoidance that are experienced by men with a darker complexion. And I and those men are unlikely to know the greater degrees of social exclusion and sometimes even outright hostility and denial of rights that are experienced by, for example, women of racial minority status who are immigrants or otherwise living experiences that are different from the norm. These experiences often create compounding challenges that are hard to address without looking at the whole picture of what a person is experiencing.

It is normal to feel sympathetic toward the goals of intersectional theory because it is definitely speaking to people's real difficulties in society. In theory, the world would be a better place if we were to honestly and seriously approach the unique difficulties that are faced by the most vulnerable among us.

But in reality, does intersectional theory create this framework for making the world a better place?

Consider these headlines:

- In 2015, the former Spokane NAACP president, who had represented herself to the public as "black," was revealed to be Caucasian.
- In August 2019, U.S. senator Elizabeth Warren publicly apologized to native American groups for her claim to indigenous ancestry.
- In March 2019, Vice magazine published an article called "White People Keep Posing As People of Color for Clout," documenting the case of George Washington University African studies professor

Jessica Klug and several other cases of white women appropriating other racial identities.

- In January 2023, "queer, indigenous" activist Kay LeClaire was discovered to not be indigenous, and then resigned a teaching post at the university of Wisconsin that had the goal of helping the public "understand the stakes of cultural appropriation for Indigenous communities."

Why would these people – white women in particular – feel a need to steal the racial and heritage identities of minority groups?

The answer is that *they were responding to incentives.*

Intersectionality shares a problem with other branches of Marxist theory, and that problem is a refusal to seriously explore the ways in which people respond to incentives.

To understand this, let's return to visualizing the Marxist narrative of society, and let's consider that with intersectionality, the private property maintained by the superstructure is privilege:

Intersectionality, Identity Politics, and the Gospel

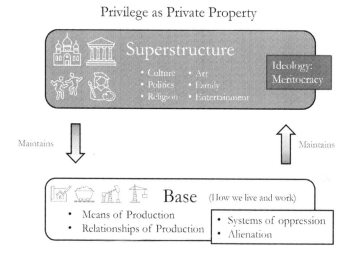

Whether intended or not, the actual effects of intersectional theory have been twofold: first, to make any forms of privilege radioactive, something like a curse. And second, to elevate experiences of marginalization and oppression to become the new signifiers of moral status in society. People who lack minority status are now told to "pass the mic" in discussions of social problems. Young people at school, particularly girls, are made to feel uninteresting and are excluded from "important conversations" when they lack the oppression status that would give them moral standing to participate.

And what do we observe stepping into this tension?

Ironically enough, just capitalism.

To illustrate how, imagine if we were to observe in America a clear trend to devalue the U.S. dollar, accompanied by a spike in the value of a cryptocurrency, bitcoin. Most of us, if we were immersed in the workings of these markets, would ask a very capitalist question:

how do I get in on that? And we would hurry to exchange dollars for bitcoin in order to use the rising bitcoin value to acquire more private property.

Similarly, people who have been immersed in the theory of intersectionality for the past two decades have seen a trend in the identity market, so to speak. This is a market trend to devalue any identity that is not marginalized, and increase the value of identities that are marginalized. People see the spike in value of marginalization and ask the question: *how do I get in on that?*

And to answer that question, whether intended or not, intersectional theory has created a market for identity-appropriation: name changes, costumes, surgeries, and more.

And let's not forget the market for intersectional entertainment. From 2009-2015, the American TV show Glee presented viewers with teen drama mixed with intersectional tension. During the show's run, teens and young adults gathered on social media site Tumblr to discuss each episode and the character dynamics of the show. Later, a user named *twelveclara* who was one of the participants in those discussions, related the experience. What follows is a censored version of her remarks:

> its not history, its blood. i still see it all over this website. the vague posts. the deactivated urls. where do u think the word problematic became popular. where do u think the representational anger started. glee was the hungry gaping void that consumed us all…
>
> and we fell for it. we watched glee and we related to its characters and we fought its wars until it was too late…
>
> character vs character, ship vs ship, blogger against blogger. We…hated each other. there was no glee fandom. there were character fandoms and ship

Intersectionality, Identity Politics, and the Gospel

fandoms and that is it...

we were consumers of the hell we created and we just kept producing more in a...dystopian fandom chain of supply and demand...

this website is a reflection of the hole glee left when it finished taking all it could from us, when the void could not consume anything more, and the posts on it now, the social justice "discourse" ... is from those who refused to learn from us. the history is here and it followed us and we can never ever escape it.[1]

Reflect for a moment on her language in that horrifying account: she referred to a "dystopian fandom chain of supply and demand." *Twelveclara* understood the market forces at work here. The TV show Glee created an intersectional hellscape in online spaces, devastating the mental and emotional health of young people, but the ratings were high enough to incentivize the show's producers to keep the show running.

When intersectional theory changes perceptions of what it means to have status, forces of capitalism are all too willing to offer consumers whatever goods and services will give them even an illusory experience of acquiring that new status.

In 2022 writer Ryan Grim wrote an article in The Intercept, entitled "Meltdowns Have Brought Progressive Advocacy Groups to a Standstill." In his article, he discussed the implosion of numerous progressive advocacy groups who were consumed with intersectional dynamics. He detailed severe conflict within the Guttmacher institute and other groups:

That the institute has spent the course of the Biden

[1] Twelveclara on Glee (Tumblr)

administration paralyzed makes it typical of not just the abortion rights community — Planned Parenthood, NARAL, Pro-Choice America, and other reproductive health organizations had similarly been locked in knock-down, drag-out fights between competing factions of their organizations, most often breaking down along staff-versus-management lines. It's also true of the progressive advocacy space across the board, which has, more or less, effectively ceased to function. The Sierra Club, Demos, the American Civil Liberties Union, Color of Change, the Movement for Black Lives, Human Rights Campaign, Time's Up, the Sunrise Movement, and many other organizations have seen wrenching and debilitating turmoil in the past couple years.[2]

Activist infighting over oppression is one of the toxic fruits of Marxist thinking, going back to the implosion of the First International under Marx's leadership.

There was recently an interesting case study of how this plays out in activist circles, as a commentator who calls himself Billboard Chris went to an anti-Israel protest wearing a sign that says "Children cannot consent to puberty blockers." Chris was confronted by an angry white male activist who called him a "fascist," and then two Muslim women approached and challenged the white male activist, supporting Billboard Chris' message critical of medical gender interventions for children. The white male activist calculated his intersectional status against the Muslim women, and being intersectionally outranked in the argument, the white male activist fled the scene.[3]

---

2 Grim, "How Meltdowns Brought Progressive Groups to a Standstill."

3 Billboard Chris, "Masked Antifa Man." (X)

When people make oppression into identity, it is a recipe for conflict. And it creates perverse incentives to race to the top of the ladder of perceived marginalization. These incentives are especially powerful among activist groups where members have been indoctrinated to believe that their hopes for a better future are only to be found in the acquisition of power.

With this understanding, we as church members can ask ourselves some honest and practical questions. Would we want to work in an environment where intersectionality is the way of establishing people's roles and status in the organization? Observing what it has done to other organizations, would we want intersectionality to become the guiding principle for our interactions at church?

How the Extremes Imitate Each Other

Finally, in discussions of intersectionality it is important to understand a concept that we will return to at several points in the next chapters: the Marxist worldview creates its own toxic mirror image at the opposite end of the political spectrum.

As Francis Fukuyama explains in his book Identity,

> The final, and perhaps most significant, problem with identity politics as currently practiced on the left is that it has stimulated the rise of identity politics on the right.[4]

Fukuyama invites readers to consider:

> how the right has adopted the language and framing of identity from the left: the idea that my particular group is being victimized, that its situation and sufferings

---

4 Fukuyama, *Identity: The Demand for Dignity and the Politics of Resentment*. p.117

are invisible to the rest of society, and that the whole of the social and political structure responsible for this situation (read: the media and political elites) needs to be smashed. Identity politics is the lens through which most social issues are now seen across the ideological spectrum.[5]

Again, when a group's goal is the acquisition of power, they will follow incentives wherever those incentives lead, even if that means imitating their enemies' successful strategies for manipulating people's moral sensibilities. Fukuyama correctly argues that leftists who are horrified and puzzled by the behavior of the extreme right, only need to look in the mirror for answers.

One of the most spiritually toxic aspects of identity politics is the price its adherents pay in diminishing their capacity for moral judgment. To be a morally developed person involves making judgments about the rightness and wrongness of things that people and institutions do. It involves affirming that some behaviors are morally acceptable and others are not.

To be sure, there is also a spiritually-healthy place for development of a sense of moral pragmatism, as when Jesus told His followers "Make to yourselves friends of the mammon of unrighteousness..." (Luke 16:9). We do not need to develop moral reflexes that are so rigid that we become incapable of working in the world as it is.

But as we will discuss throughout this book, when we find ourselves excusing criminality and adultery and murder among our identity tribe, that is a sign that identity politics has warped our moral sensibilities to the point that we are no longer exercising agency in the way that God

---

5   Ibid., p. 122

intends. In the scriptures, the word for this is *damnation*. It is a term that indicates our progress toward eternal life is halted.

Denial of Moral Agency

In a fascinating blog post, Arnold Kling discusses a metaphor of babies and robots in our thinking about morality and agency. He references the book The Mind Club by Daniel Wegner and Kurt Gray:

> Wegner and Gray see a baby and a robot as occupying opposite ends of the spectrum of incomplete minds. The baby lacks the ability to plan and make choices. The robot lacks the ability to feel sensations and emotions.

Kling quotes the authors giving examples:

> Imagine that the baby and the robot were just about to tumble off a cliff and you could save only one of them. Which would you save? Likely you would save the baby… imagine that the baby and the robot have found a loaded gun and are playing with it, when it goes off and injures someone. Which of them would you hold responsible? If you're like most people you would forgive the baby and condemn the robot to the junkyard.

Kling then explains that Wegner and Gray "call this combination of an innocent feeler and a guilty doer the moral dyad. It consists of an agent and a patient, an intentional thinking doer and a suffering vulnerable feeler."[6]

The robot and baby metaphor is an excellent way of understanding how identity politics shuts down our moral development. We begin to see ourselves and people in our

---

6   Kling, "Two Theories of Mind."

identity group as the innocent babies incapable of doing wrong, and people in rival identity groups as the oppressive robots who hold all the agency and all the capacity for evil.

These are the fruits of identity politics. The behaviors of certain people and classes of people become immune from any kind of moral evaluation. We surrender our moral reasoning in order to get particular people in power, and the price we pay is our soul, and the price we pay is also the faith of our children who become disillusioned with religion after observing religious people's willingness to constantly suspend their moral reasoning in the hopes of political gain.

One of the most notorious exploiters of identity politics for evil was Russian dictator Josef Stalin, who was also one of the most prolific mass murderers in history. In historical footage of Stalin's Moscow meetings with Western leaders in 1942, we see a contrast in clothing, with Western leaders wearing nice suits and uniforms, while Stalin wore a simple worker's uniform. The intended effect was simple: Stalin was showing his people that he was *one of them*. Here he was among the world's great leaders, but he was representing the little guy, the common worker. In his choice of clothing, Stalin was speaking to the identity intuitions of the left, and making himself immune to moral evaluation of any kind. His unspoken message to ordinary Russians was "I might be a monster, but the only thing that matters is that I'm *your* monster."

Of course, Stalin's real lifestyle was not that of a common worker; it was that of a wealthy dictator. When Marx spoke of the need for a dictatorship of the proletariat, he probably did not envision Stalin's regime, which killed millions of poor Russians. But nevertheless, Stalin's regime was one of the horrifying fruits of the Marxist worldview.

The Gospel Approach

With all of this in mind, it is important to acknowledge that in the restored gospel there is a righteous and inspired understanding of what it means to be vulnerable in society, and how society should care for the vulnerable. In the Old Testament, the most common divine commandment to the ancient Israelites was to take care of the foreigners living among them. In other passages of scripture, we see language directing care for other vulnerable groups, such as widows, the fatherless, and the poor.

It is abundantly clear from scripture that God expects His people to create a society that cares for specific disadvantaged groups of people. This has always been part of Israel's mission as God's people, to model for the rest of humanity God's ideal vision of how His children should live in the world.

In our honest assessment of the awful consequences of intersectional thinking and identity politics, we do not become absolved of our own gospel responsibilities to find ways to make society better for the disadvantaged, and if we are concerned about destructive Marxist social justice movements based in intersectionality and identity politics, we would benefit from giving even more attention to promoting a positive and gospel-centered vision of caring for the most vulnerable in society.

Chapter 4

Critical Race Theory and the Gospel

In 2020, when Critical Race Theory (CRT) was increasingly becoming a focus of conversation in American politics, I read Richard Delgado and Jean Stefancic's book *Critical Race Theory: An Introduction*. Having heard about CRT primarily through conversations online, I approached the book with nervousness. It is considered a core text for familiarizing people with the basics of CRT, and given the tension surrounding CRT, I expected to read something very controversial.

I was surprised to find that I agreed with many things in that book.

That might be upsetting to readers who understand the problems with critical race theory, and we will take an unflinching and honest look at those problems as we proceed. But first, we need to explore some of the core principles that are presented in the book.

CRT began primarily as an academic effort in legal studies to examine how law creates and reinforces systemic racism. But as Delgado and Stefancic acknowledge, CRT has spread into other fields including education and political science. They provide an alarming synopsis of CRT's approach: "Unlike traditional civil rights, which embraces incrementalism and step-by-step progress, critical race theory questions the very foundations of the liberal order, including equality theory, legal reasoning, Enlightenment rationalism, and neutral principles of constitutional law."[1]

This synopsis is alarming because when people cannot agree on some basic sense of what is rational, conversations can be full of wild false claims about reality and every interaction between people becomes a chess match with power as the goal. Reasoning and rationality provide a set of rules that everyone can agree to, that allow for some amount of productive engagement between human beings who hold different views. Without them, people tend toward conflict.

Also, the rejection of neutral principles of constitutional law leads to an abandonment of fairness as a guiding principle in the legal system, which likewise leads to conflict. A clear example of this was recently seen in Chicago, where the city decided to resettle thousands of undocumented immigrants from Central and South America. In the Chicago Sun-Times, Alderman Desmon Yancy wrote,

> Our streets are crumbling, our storefronts are vacant, our neighborhoods are unsafe, young people are hopeless and our elders are losing their homes. So many neighborhoods that are not on the South and West sides are thriving, and we can't get any relief. The pain

---

[1] Delgado and Stefancic, *Critical Race Theory: An Introduction, Second Edition*. (Kindle Locations 142-144)

> couldn't be any more obvious.
>
> Now, the migrant issue has been placed right in the laps of these same Black folks. Thousands of migrants have been resettled in Black neighborhoods, and the city, county and state developed a plan to support them.
>
> As part of that plan, City Council members were asked last month to support a new $70 million investment in our migrant mission that, coupled with money from the state and county, will equal $300 million. This investment felt like a strong-arm robbery when you consider the meager investments Black leaders have asked for and been denied.[2]

Alderman Yancy was describing the frustration felt by Chicago residents over a problem that they did not cause. Immigration is a matter of Federal law, and whenever the federal government decides that border security is not important, this decision imposes a real burden upon black communities. This reality was recently explained by African-American schoolteacher and activist Gregg Marcel Dixon:

> Immigration to the United States since 1965 has almost quadrupled. This second "Great Wave" of immigration to America has done great harm to Black Americans, much as the flood of immigration from Europe following the Civil War did. According to a study by economists from Harvard and the University of Chicago, the influx of new immigrants between 1980 and 2000 accounts for as much as 60 percent of the decline in wages, 25 percent of the decline in employment rates, and 10 percent of the increase in incarceration rates among less-educated

---

2   Yancy, "Why so Many Black Chicagoans Are Frustrated by the Migrant Crisis - Chicago Sun-Times."

Blacks.[3]

What Dixon describes is a systemic problem, one that exists at the level of America's immigration system established and maintained by the federal government. By contrast, Dixon explains that formerly, America's immigration system worked in favor of black workers:

> In 1924, House Democrats voted 158-37 to drastically slash immigration. A. Philip Randolph, one of the most prominent Black labor and civil rights leaders of the day, praised the restrictions, explaining that too much immigration "over-floods the labor market, resulting in lowering the standard of living." As the flood of competing foreign workers slowed to a trickle, Black workers made gains. Frank Morris, the former executive director of the Congressional Black Caucus Foundation, noted that Black men's wages quadrupled from 1940 to 1980, growing even faster than white wages.

A core element of Critical Race Theory is the power of personal stories, as opposed to traditional forms of academic research. But in the case of immigration and its impact on black communities, we see one of the many areas where CRT undermines itself.

Whose personal stories are to be heard and valued? Those of immigrants who have arrived in the U.S. illegally? Or the voices of African Americans who are adversely impacted by the influx of immigrants to their communities? When intersectional theory makes marginalization into the basis for policy, there are choices to make about who is the most marginalized. And when we abandon reason and rationality, choices about how

---

[3] Dixon, "When It Comes to Immigration Reform, Don't Forget Black Voters | Opinion - Newsweek."

we rank people's marginalization turn out to be arbitrary choices between stories, choices of whose narratives of oppression to believe, made by whoever is in power, however poorly they understand the communities they are affecting.

Whiteness and White Supremacy

Returning from discussion of policy back to discussion of theory, the Marxist nature of CRT is illustrated in how CRT treats "whiteness" as the private property[4] that forms the basis for oppression and marginalization:

Whiteness as Private Property

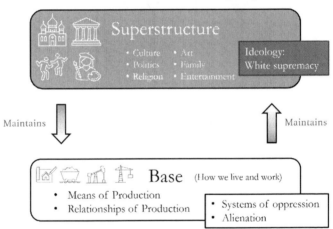

Also in this Marxist template, we see white supremacy as the ideology that is employed to maintain the system.

With these references to whiteness and white supremacy, we arrive at one of the primary problems with critical race theory: it is a totalizing set of explanations

---

4   Note: the notion of whiteness as property was explained by Cheryl Harris in the Harvard Law Review in 1993.

Critical Race Theory and the Gospel

for how the world works. Totalizing means that CRT eventually comes to be the answer for questions about everything that is wrong with the world. For example,

- When Tyre Nichols was killed in 2023 by five black police officers, their actions were attributed to white supremacy.[5]
- In 2020, the Earth Island Institute published an article called "How White Supremacy Caused the Climate Crisis."[6]
- In 2021, in an attempt to explain racial minorities' support for Trump, NPR published a story on "Understanding Multiracial Whiteness And Trump Supporters."[7]
- A 2007 academic study concluded that in contrast with the industrial systems of food production common in the United States, "whiteness is produced in progressive non-profit efforts to promote sustainable farming and food security."[8]

Yes, you read that last one correctly. Progressive non-profits that promote sustainable farming and food security are *producing whiteness*. This is the quality of thinking that emerges when a theory has no guardrails of rationality: in this case, whiteness and white supremacy have become a catch-all accusatory label for *everything in the world that we don't like*.

---

5 "Rep. Jamaal Bowman Raising Money off the 'White Supremacy' That Killed Tyre Nichols."

6 Grudin, "How White Supremacy Caused the Climate Crisis."

7 "Understanding Multiracial Whiteness And Trump Supporters."

8 Conrad, "Identifying and Countering White Supremacy Culture in Food Systems."

In 2020 there went viral a clip from a meeting of a school board in Virginia, where an African-American mother gave a heated tirade against the teaching of CRT in schools. She claimed that CRT was racist, abusive, and that it had been used in the past to dumb down her ancestors.[9] If that assessment sounds extreme, also consider that in 2020 The National Museum of African American History & Culture published an infographic on "aspects and assumptions of whiteness and white culture in the united states," that identified among other things, self-reliance, the nuclear family, rationality, hard work, respect for authority, and delayed gratification.

When these basic ingredients for resilient character and life success are being characterized as whiteness (and therefore evil), it is easy to see why parents would be extremely nervous at the possibility that their children would be indoctrinated into this new way of thinking.

In a 2023 article I wrote for Public Square Magazine, I wrote that empathy tends to have an honesty problem.[10] Critical Race Theorist Richard Delgado agrees, and in an academic paper, he criticized empathy and also invoked Antonio Gramsci's idea of "false consciousness," where an oppressed person adopts the views of their oppressor.[11] In Delgado's framing, when a white person feels empathy toward someone who is a racial minority, their empathy is self-interested. The white person will always try to help in ways that reflect the white person's own understanding of what is helpful. And in another principle of CRT called

---

9   YouTube, "Furious Mother Slams Her Children's School Board for Enforcing Critical Race Theory."

10 Ellsworth, "Empathy in Modern Culture."

11 Delgado, "Rodrigo's Eleventh Chronicle."

"interest convergence," white people offer help when their personal interests converge with those of the people they are helping.

These sound like very cynical ways of looking at humanity, but often they are factually true. Comedy team Key and Peele have a hilarious skit called "Awkward Apologies from White People" that highlights this in a humorous way.[12] Perhaps the most visible example of this problem is the work of Robin DiAngelo, a "critical whiteness educator" who gains income from doing speaking engagements and seminars on race.

In DiAngelo's book White Fragility, she offers that "…a positive white identity is an impossible goal. White identity is inherently racist; white people do not exist outside the system of white supremacy."[13] Tomiwa Olowade calls White Fragility "self-help for narcissistic white people," and his critique of the book is accurate. He notices the book's "Lutheran-like emphasis on the need to purge yourself of racism,"[14] which is an essential insight, because what DiAngelo offers readers is new religion, including a new form of religious scrupulosity. She adopts a notion commonly held in Christian groups – the notion of original sin – but sees it in terms of racism.

White Fragility teaches essentially that a white person is born into a worldwide system of racial oppression that was conceived in the original sin of whiteness, but when our eyes are opened we are awakened to our inherent

---

12 YouTube, Key & Peele, "Awkward Apologies from White People"

13 DiAngelo and Dyson, *White Fragility: Why It's So Hard for White People to Talk About Racism*. p.149

14 Owolade, "Antiracism Won't Save You: Robin DiAngelo's New Book Is Self-Help for Narcissistic White People."

sinfulness and the "fallen" structurally-inequitable nature of the world around us. DiAngelo offers her version of repentance and discipleship in this new religious worldview:

> I strive to be "less white." To be less white is to be less racially oppressive. This requires me to be more racially aware, to be better educated about racism, and to continually challenge racial certitude and arrogance.[15]

Robin DiAngelo puts her readers into a situation called a *Kafka trap*, which is commonly employed in discussions by critical race theorists. The term *Kafka trap* is derived from Franz Kafka's book *The Trial*, where a character is apprehended and put on trial, and all of his denials and resistance to the accusations are taken as evidence of his guilt. The logic of a Kafka trap is, *John is guilty of x* **because he denies being guilty of x**. *Denials of guilt of x are* **evidence that someone is guilty** *of x*. Kafka traps are common in conspiracy thinking as well: *powerful people are conspiring to do x, and John expressed skepticism of their conspiracy. That makes John part of the conspiracy.* The goal of the Kafka trap is simple: it is to condemn and shame a person, regardless of their moral guilt or innocence.

The title of Robin DiAngelo's book, White Fragility, is the opening to the Kafka trap. Then she fully traps the reader with a number of claims, including

- "Racism and our involvement in it cannot be avoided" (p.224)
- "From an antiracist perspective, the question is not, 'Did racism take place' but 'How was racism

---

15   DiAngelo and Dyson, *White Fragility*, p.149

Critical Race Theory and the Gospel

taking place' because the assumption is that racism is always at play, always operating." (p.330)

- White-fragile responses to antiracist messaging include feeling "singled out," "attacked," "silenced," "shamed," "guilty," "accused," "insulted," "judged," "angry," "scared," or "outraged." (p.119)
- White fragile behaviors in response to those feelings include "crying," "physically leaving," "emotionally withdrawing," "arguing," "denying," "focusing on intentions," "seeking absolution," and "avoiding." (p.119)

It is clear that there literally is no acceptable response other than a stoical acceptance of this new indoctrination. Any other response is fragility that perpetuates the sin of racism. This is a classic Kafka trap.

The "antiracism" taught by Robin DiAngelo is self-obsessive. White Fragility reads like the personal story of someone who is consumed with self-loathing and absolutely terrified of being perceived by others as an unrepentant sinner. Tomiwa Olowade's review of the book concludes,

> In the end, it is supposed to be about the individual white person overcoming a barrier to greater racial enlightenment. In truth, what is offered is not enlightenment but an emotionally and intellectually enervating form of narcissism.[16]

---

16 Owolade, "Antiracism Won't Save You: Robin DiAngelo's New Book Is Self-Help for Narcissistic White People."

Epistemology is Everything

We mentioned earlier the importance of personal stories in Critical Race Theory, and this is a profoundly important concept to understand.

Epistemology is the study of knowledge: how we arrive at things we believe, things we know, and why we differentiate between those two. Religious epistemology – the way we arrive at our religious beliefs – is different from the epistemology employed in social sciences (like psychology and sociology), and social sciences use different epistemology than, say, the field of music history. There is not one single epistemology that covers all of these fields, because these fields are all asking different kinds of questions.

Personal stories are extremely important in religious epistemology, where we are asking questions like

- Is there a God?
- How does God work among humanity?
- How is revelation experienced?

..and more questions that cannot be answered through scientific epistemology. In religious epistemology, we rely mainly on personal stories found in scripture, and personal stories found among believers in the present day. We call these stories *testimony*. When we see patterns emerge in testimony of believers who are speaking with sound minds, we become more and more confident that these people are telling the truth about something that is real.

When it comes to making law and policies that affect large groups of people, however, personal stories are only one part of epistemology.

To illustrate why, imagine that I am the mayor of a large city, and in a town hall meeting, one of the racial-minority residents of the city tells me that the city has a severe problem of air pollution. The conversation then goes like this:

Me: I have not observed a problem of air pollution in the city. What makes you think that we have this problem?

Resident: I am living it.

Me: Tell me about that, please.

Resident: I wake up and there is smoky air around my house, almost every day.

Me: Where do you live?

Resident: I live in the Northwestern corner, near the canyon.

With this, let's suppose that I as mayor assign one of my staff to get in touch with this resident, and go and visit his neighborhood. My staffer returns and informs me that the resident is part of a small, mostly racial-minority neighborhood where the layout of the land is such that breezes converge and bring smoke from other areas of the city, and sometimes that smoke stays for days at a time until there is a windy day that cleans the air.

In this case, as I figure out how to respond to my resident, I need to make decisions of epistemology. Do I accept this resident's sincerely-felt view that the whole city has a problem of air pollution, and then make a sweeping policy decision that impacts the entire city? Or do I ask more questions?

For example, let's suppose that some of the smoke impacting my resident is coming from poor neighborhoods that rely upon the burning of firewood for heating.

Or, suppose that the smoke is coming from a mostly-immigrant neighborhood that cooks food in a way that generates a lot of smoke. As I ponder policy options to help my constituents, I might need to make value judgments between two different communities. And I will need to make a decision of epistemology: do I want to see if there is a scientific question in this situation, requiring scientific study of location and wind patterns and population? Or do I just want to alleviate a small minority community's frustration, no matter how it impacts everyone else?

In every human circumstance where the truth matters, epistemology is everything.

…Which brings us to an article by philosophy professor Alison Bailey, called "Tracking Privilege-Preserving Epistemic Pushback in Feminist and Critical Race Philosophy Classes". That title is daunting, but let's translate it into ordinary language. "Epistemic pushback" is when we push back on someone's decisions around epistemology. If I claim that water on my stove will start to boil at 500 degrees Fahrenheit because that's how I feel in my heart, and a scientist tells me that no, the water will boil at 212 degrees Fahrenheit and I can verify that using a thermometer, the scientist is giving me epistemic pushback. He is telling me that feelings in my heart are the wrong epistemology to determine when the water on my stove will boil, and that using a thermometer is the epistemology that will show me what is true.

So, when Dr. Bailey refers to privilege-preserving epistemic pushback, she is saying that sometimes people challenge others' choices around epistemology in order to preserve privilege, and the title of her paper points to this happening in "critical race philosophy classes". Dr. Bailey says the following in her paper:

Critical Race Theory and the Gospel

> Critical pedagogy [the teaching of critical race theory] begins from ***a different set of assumptions rooted in the neo-Marxian literature on critical theory commonly associated with the Frankfurt School***. Here, the critical learner is someone who is empowered and motivated to seek justice and emancipation. Critical pedagogy regards the claims that students make in response to social-justice issues ***not as propositions to be assessed for their truth value***, but as expressions of power that function to reinscribe and perpetuate social inequality.[17] (emphasis added)

I added emphasis in this quote, because here she is saying some really important things about the teaching of CRT. She is using her paper to explain that some students have a hard time with discussions of CRT – and offer pushback – because they are not operating from the neo-Marxist epistemology that is at the heart of CRT. And in those discussions, claims that students make are not to be evaluated as to whether or not they are true.

Take a moment to imagine a classroom environment where the truth of people's claims is irrelevant. Instead of thinking about whether a statement is true, you are to only consider whether it shifts power in a particular way.

If that sounds like a recipe for disaster, it is. It is a classroom full of Kafka traps, where pushback in the interest of truth means that a student is complicit in a conspiracy to maintain privilege and white supremacy.

In 2016, an award-winning black economist at Harvard University, Roland Fryer, published a study analyzing police shootings in the United States to find if there is evidence of racial bias in police shootings of African

---

17   Bailey, "Tracking Privilege-Preserving Epistemic Pushback in Feminist and Critical Race Philosophy Classes."

Americans. Fryer understood the importance of personal perspective, so in preparation for his research, he traveled to several places and went on numerous ride-alongs with police officers to observe how policing works in black communities.

Analyzing data on police use of force, Fryer came to a conclusion that challenged the narrative that police shootings reflect bias against African Americans. He had been using eight research assistants who worked on the data analysis for a year, and when he saw the results of the analysis, he hired eight new research assistants and asked them to analyze the data anew. When they independently arrived at a similar result, he assembled the final product: a 104-page analysis with a 150-page appendix of supporting data.

Fryer encountered fierce hostility toward his paper before it was even published, and when he published the paper, the hostility became personally directed at him, to the point where he needed armed guards to accompany him everywhere for more than a month.

Ibram Kendi famously claimed that "One either allows racial inequities to persevere, as a racist, or confronts racial inequities, as an anti-racist. There is no in-between safe space of 'not racist.'"[18] This kind of thinking may help to explain the hostility faced by Roland Fryer and others who sincerely seek to develop research studies that accurately reflect reality, rather than studies that might advance a predetermined view of racial policy remedies, without concern for whether the information is actually true. In the minds of critical theorists, an acclaimed black economist like Roland Fryer who is actively working

---

18 Kendi, *How to Be an Antiracist*. p.10

to better black lives in countless ways through his professional and philanthropic work, is still a racist if he communicates realities that reside outside of a particular activist narrative.

The choice to abandon rationality for ideologically-driven policy messaging has real consequences, some of which create real harm for minority communities. In his book *San Fransicko: Why Progressives Ruin Cities*, former socialist activist Michael Shellenberger wrote, "Too often progressive idealism creates greater loyalty to a highly romanticized view, one that allowed progressives to justify defunding and shutting down core institutions..."[19]

For an example, recall the American racial turmoil of 2020 and consider the policy proposal advanced during that time, to "defund the police." Numerous cities did exactly that, reducing funds to their police forces in response to activist messaging. In a New York Times report titled "How 'defund the police' failed," we read of the consequences of that policy in Minneapolis:

> As police ranks thinned out, violent crime soared. Gang violence, once a modest problem in Minneapolis, became such a challenge that federal prosecutors charged 45 people suspected of being gang members in a pair of racketeering indictments in May, a first in the city.
>
> Many residents have given up on the local public transportation system, where some stations increasingly have become gathering points for people who openly smoke fentanyl and other drugs. The number of car thefts and carjackings skyrocketed. As of early June, more than 4,100 vehicles had been stolen in the city this

---

19 Shellenberger, *San Fransicko: Why Progressives Ruin Cities*. pp.273-274

year, nearly twice as many as during the same period last year.[20]

The New York Times would later report on the reversal of defunding in police departments around the country, in response to surging rates of violent crime that disproportionately harmed African American communities.[21]

Beyond harmful failed policies, the fruits of Critical Race Theory are similar to those of other neo-Marxist movements: they are emotional extortion, interpersonal conflict, and bullying. This was seen in the 2023 implosion of Ibram Kendi's Center for Antiracism at Boston University, as former employee Yanique Redwood described the center's atmosphere of "anxiety, stress, anger, and fear."[22] The practical effect of this is to cause most people to simply disengage from activism. After all, if participation in a movement is going to lead a person into a stream of constant accusatory abuse and shaming, the movement does not value objective truth, and the institutions of the movement are interpersonal conflict zones, then, well, most people simply don't have an appetite for that kind of exhausting self-punishment.

Does the restored gospel offer better possibilities? I believe so, and in what follows I will offer reasons for that belief. But there is no escaping the fact that this is going to be a hard conversation.

20　Londoño, "How 'Defund the Police' Failed"

21　Goodman, "A Year After 'Defund,' Police Departments Get Their Money Back."

22　Andreae, "Trouble Was Already Brewing at Kendi's Anti-Racism Center in 2021."

A Gospel Perspective on Critical Race Theory

In Delgado and Stefancic's book Critical Race Theory, they tell a story that resonated with something I experienced on my mission in Brazil. Delgado and Stefancic provide an excerpt from an appeals court ruling where a parent had filed a complaint against a school district over class readings that contained racial epithets. The appeals court explained,

> In her amended complaint, Monteiro alleged that her ninth grade daughter and other similarly situated African-American students attended a school where they were called [the n word] by white children, and where that term was written on the walls of the buildings in which they were supposed to learn civics and social studies. It does not take an educational psychologist to conclude that being referred to by one's peers by the most noxious racial epithet in the contemporary American lexicon, being shamed and humiliated on the basis of one's race, and having the school authorities ignore or reject one's complaints would adversely affect a Black child's ability to obtain the same benefit from schooling as her white counterparts. . . . It is the beginning of high school, when a young adolescent is highly impressionable and is making decisions about education that will affect the course of her life. . . . [A] school where this sort of conduct occurs unchecked is utterly failing in its mandate to provide a nondiscriminatory educational environment.[23]

In this situation, a mother's legal complaint was describing a kind of tax that her daughter and other black students were having to pay on an ongoing basis as they

---

23 Delgado and Stefancic, *Critical Race Theory* (Kindle locations 446-453)

attended the school. It might be hard for white students and parents to imagine the psychological and emotional tax that would come with going to school and being constantly racially denigrated, because we do not pay that tax. But just imagining living in that circumstance, we can sense how that tax would result in a reduced ability to focus in class, to maintain a healthy cognitive state while on school grounds, and ultimately, to benefit from education.

For these reasons, I am very much in agreement with the appeals court's rulings in favor of the child's mother.

To help illustrate how this can apply to our church experience, on my mission in Brazil in 1994, I served in an area where the bishop of the local ward and his wife (I'll call her Maria) were both Brazilians of African descent. I became very close to that family; our lunch appointments became fun times for gospel discussion and playing with their kids. One day at lunch after the kids left the table, Maria got quiet and serious, and asked me a hard question:

"Elder Ellsworth, do you think I was less faithful in premortality?"

I sat there disturbed, not knowing what to say. At some point I had heard a vague notion that some church members believed the reason for the priesthood ban toward members of African descent was based on the fact that those members had been less than faithful in premortality, and therefore had come to earth in African lineages that would leave them without the priesthood.

I had never given much thought to that idea, but here was a remarkable member of the church sitting before me, clearly impacted by it. Before, this speculative explanation for race had been just an abstract idea to me. Now, it was real, affecting someone I regarded as a personal friend.

Critical Race Theory and the Gospel

I responded to Maria with my gut feeling. I said no, she had not been less than faithful in premortality, and whoever believed that was wrong. I could see a visible sense of relief come over her.

But imagine the mental, emotional, and spiritual tax that Maria had been paying day after day, year after year, knowing that some members of her community believed these erroneous things about her premortal faithfulness. Imagine constantly paying the tax of knowing that some members of the church who are regarded as knowledgeable in scripture, have ways of justifying and reinforcing beliefs that denigrate your soul. Imagine going to church and seeing people around you and constantly wondering if they believe these things about you.

These experiences, and many others, function like spiritual taxes that limit minorities' ability to experience community well, and also limit the ability of everyone in the church to perceive God's understanding of reality.

To eliminate these taxes upon the membership of the church, we need not embrace the shaming and delusions and bullying tactics of Marxist movements. The elimination of these taxes is something that we do not because we are hopelessly depraved and sinful, but because we are good. We are blood and spirit descendants of pioneers who did very hard things that were asked of them. We can work to eliminate race-based cultural taxes upon the church because it is our magnificent heritage to rise to challenges.

In Critical Race Theory there is effort expended to revise the past to increase the sense of shame that nations feel about their history. In the church, there is no need to revise the past. We can honestly acknowledge racist views that have been held by figures in our past, and we can ask a powerful question: what do those souls believe now?

When people translate things from one language to another, there are different *translation theories*, different approaches to translating a text. The most obvious approach to translation is to ask the question *what did this individual want to express to their audience, and how can I translate that into another language?* But another way of thinking about translation is that the goal of translation is to *convey the mind of the author*. For that, we ask different questions: *What does this individual want me to understand from their experience? What do they want me to learn from them, now, in the present?* This should be the healing and redeeming translation theory that we apply to scripture and history in the church.

When I look at passages of scripture, my key to interpretation is to ask questions that are very much focused in the present. Whatever Nephi or Mormon or Paul or Moses may have thought in the past, *what is their message to me now?* And I guarantee you that none of the impressions that emerge in response to those questions are racist impressions. There is not a single prophet or other figure in scripture from the past that wishes to impose a racial tax upon any members of the church in the present day. And that means when we make decisions around the selection and translation and interpretation of sacred texts, we should do so in a way that honors their present wishes.

None of this approach requires revisionist history; it only requires openness to revelation: first, revelation that has come through our modern prophets that we need to root out racism from the church; and second, revelation about how to understand and convey to others that all prophets past and present are now united in this truth, and all of our communications about scripture and sacred history should reflect this.

Another approach that avoids the temptation of revisionist history is to learn to *grieve*. When Jews read their scripture, they read of historical figures who sometimes erred, and sometimes behaved in ways that were misguided. It would have been easy for ancient Israelite scribes to modify scripture in ways that remove all mistakes and sins from every figure in scripture, but they didn't. They kept those things in scripture, allowing future generations to lament these sad parts of Israelite history as we also rejoice in God's blessings for them.

To lament and grieve our sins and the sins of people of the past who we revere, is a righteous impulse. In the Book of Mormon, Moroni counsels readers to "Condemn me not because of mine imperfection, neither my father, because of his imperfection, neither them who have written before him; but rather give thanks unto God that he hath made manifest unto you our imperfections, that ye may learn to be more wise than we have been." (Moroni 9:31). To learn wisdom is a recurring theme in the Book of Mormon, and here Moroni offers the insight that we can learn wisdom by gratefully and gracefully learning from other people's imperfections.

We can grieve without condemning. We can honestly recognize sad parts of our and other people's history without wallowing and obsessing and engaging in the kinds of narcissistic, performative behaviors that have become typical activist responses to critical theory.

There are many other things that can be done to reduce and eliminate the burdensome and unnecessary "taxes" paid by minority communities in the church, and every church member is empowered to seek to do their part in this work.

The challenge in doing so, is to not let activism become our new religion. In a recent presentation on change in the church, I described something I have observed on social media: that when church members embrace activism to an excessive degree, they undergo a shift in their communications, from faith and testimony to demands and disillusionment:

Expressions of faith:
- I feel God's presence.
- I feel healing through the atonement of Christ.
- I acted on a prompting to minister and it turned out to be exactly what the person was seeking.
- I received a prompting while doing family history.
- I'm getting profound insights from the scriptures.
- I had real communion with God at church/in the temple.
- I sense the goodness and potential of church leaders and members, even with our shortcomings.

Activist messaging:
- Other people need to change.
- Institutions need to change.
- It's critically urgent that we put a certain person in power.
- My political candidate will achieve God's vision for society.
- I can't be at peace until a political or religious system becomes different from how it is.
- Someone is wrong and needs to be shamed.
- I'm disgusted with the people around me who don't share my views.

It is hard to say which comes first: activism or deconversion. But this problem is easily observable among members of the church, especially members with shallow roots in the gospel. A converted Latter-day Saint will have much better resources for impacting the church in a positive way, compared to deconverted members who tend to lash out and find themselves surprised when other members don't respond well to activist demands.

Finally, as we think about Critical Race Theory in relation to the gospel, there is a classic question that we always need to raise: *which way do we face?*

It is very common and predictable for a university student to gain some exposure to Marxist critical theory, and then lacking either the ability or the courage to think critically about it, they swallow it whole. It becomes their new way of seeing the world, including the church. The student then evaluates all of their church experience, and all church policies, against their theory in order to determine their value. They stand with their theory and face the church.

The reverse should be true. A Latter-day Saint student should be able to stand in Christ's restored church and face theories from that standpoint, asking questions of theories to evaluate them against gospel principles using gospel epistemology.

Doing this, I personally find much to respect and even agree with in Critical Race Theory. But I view it critically, and I would never allow it to become a totalizing worldview that supersedes the restored gospel. The differences in assumptions and epistemology between the restored gospel and critical race theory are too great for these two systems to be reconcilable.

Chapter 5

Gender Theory, Queer Theory, and the Gospel

Queer is a word that is hard to define, and this is by design. But broadly speaking, queer theory finds the idea of "normal" to be psychologically oppressive, and socially exclusive, so any elements of society that promote norms of any kind are considered to be parts of a system of oppression.

People who have long assumed that the term "queer" is a synonym for gay, lesbian, or bisexual might be surprised to learn that queer is not a synonym for gay, lesbian, bisexual, or anything else, as a gay writer explains:

> I am not queer. I am a gay man. And I do not buy the notion that "gay" must automatically be grouped into or conflated with the label of "queer." The former is not the same as or even a subgroup of the latter. In fact, in many respects, the identities of gay and queer stand in direct opposition to each other. Like the host of the podcast, most people typically never bother to ask me how I identify. They learn that I am gay, and they simply assume that makes me queer. It does not.

Until recently, I never thought it necessary to define

Gender Theory, Queer Theory, and the Gospel

"gay" or "man," but when I say that I am gay, I mean that I am same-sex attracted; when I say that I am a man, I mean that I am an adult male.

...These definitions, it turns out, are important, because contemporary queer ideology does not necessarily accept them. In fact, it seeks to disrupt and deconstruct them.[1]

With this statement, we see how queer ideology fits into the Marxist worldview:

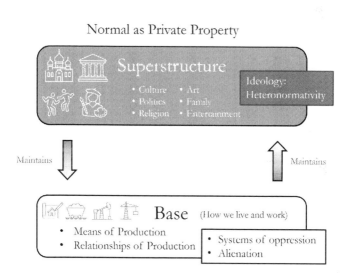

To understand how this is manifest in activism, consider the recent experience of Fred Sargeant. In September 2022, longtime gay activist Fred Sargeant went to a Burlington Vermont pride parade, where he was attacked. Here is his report on Facebook following the incident:

---

1   Gajdics, "Gay Not Queer."

Chapter 5

Mugged at Burlington Pride

> So, I went to Pride to protest their misogyny, homophobia, exclusionary policies and divisiveness. I was met by screaming, multiple assaults, ageist comments, shoving, slaps to the back of my head, pouring coffee on me and repeated attempts to steal my signs. Being unsuccessful in their attempts to disrupt my protest and drive me away, the mob pushed me to the ground as the parade ended, further injuring me. They stole or damaged more than $550 worth of my property.[2]

Reading Sargeant's account, we might assume that he was attacked by right-wing activists of one group or another, but in reality his attackers were queer activists. The activists were offended by signs he was displaying at the event, one of which read "Gay Not Queer."

Later, Sargeant offered a statement on the Disaffected podcast:

> My name is Fred Sargeant. I have been a lifelong gay rights advocate and activist. I joined the gay rights movement before the Stonewall Riots...
>
> In the fall of 1969, four of us went on to propose and then organize the very first Pride march, which was not a parade. No floats, no corporations and no massed contingents of drag queens and other fetishists, which is precisely what Burlington Pride has become...
>
> Burlington Pride has now become a platform for misogyny, exclusion and hate. "Gay" is now defined by the Pride Center of Vermont as a term of erasure; no member of their team or board identifies as gay, just as queer. Queer theory seeks not only to erase societal norms and values, it seeks to erase LGB people from the movement that they created.

---

2   Sargeant, "Mugged at Burlington Pride."

> ...I have likened the present LGBTQ+ movement to a marriage gone terribly bad. The TQ+ part has become irreversibly domineering and abusive. And like all such chronically abusive relationships, beyond repair. Our interests are too different.[3]

The queer movement clearly follows the neo-Marxist pattern of critical theory employed against a perceived system of oppression, but there are more nuances to the Marxist leanings of the movement, and they are best expressed in the words of some of its notable figures.

How Queer Theorists Claim Marxism

In his book "The Reification of Desire: Toward a Queer Marxism," author Kevin Lloyd recounts a gathering of Marxist activists where the speaker was one of the founding figures of the queer movement, Judith Butler. Butler's remarks became a published essay called "merely cultural,"[4] and Butler's intention was to explore a tension within Marxist circles between those whose Marxist concerns are focused on material factors like economic class, versus cultural factors like sexuality.

Challenging Marxists who focus entirely on economics and class struggle, Butler wrote:

> Why would a movement concerned to criticize and transform the ways in which sexuality is socially regulated not be understood as central to the functioning of political economy? Indeed, that this critique and transformation is central to the project of materialism was the trenchant point made by socialist feminists

---

3   MathNerd, "Statement from Fred Sargeant."

4   Butler, "Merely Cultural."

and those interested in the convergence of Marxism and psychoanalysis in the 1970s and 1980s, and was clearly inaugurated by Engels and Marx with their own insistence that 'mode of production' needed to include forms of social association. In The German Ideology (1846), Marx famously wrote, 'men, who daily remake their own life, begin to make other men, to propagate their kind: the relation between man and woman, parents and children, the family.'[5]

In other words, Butler is sending a message that cultural Marxism (including queer theory) is every bit as vital, every bit as essential to the core vision of Marx as are any materialist economic concerns. Sometimes in what is called "orthodox Marxism" the entire vision of Marxism is understood to be communism, the abolition of private property and class distinctions. But here Butler emphatically argues that cultural Marxism is fully orthodox as well. Butler even uses Antonio Gramsci's notion of hegemony to confront other activists on the left:

> How quickly we forget that new social movements based on democratic principles became articulated against a hegemonic Left as well as a complicitous liberal centre and a truly threatening right wing?[6]

In this quote we can see the heart of the conflict between queer theory and the LGB movement: queer theorists see the norms of of the LGB movement – such as clear definitions for terms, and adherence to the sex binary of male and female – as a hegemonic system of oppression.

Butler's reference to the family is very important as well, since Marx and his colleague Engels were very hostile

---

5   Ibid.

6   Ibid.

Gender Theory, Queer Theory, and the Gospel

to the family.[7] For Butler to mention the family in this way sent another signal to her Marxist audience that queer theory is aligned with core Marxist objectives.

Pinning Jello to a Wall: Defining Queer

Well, if queer theory is *against* both the family and the basic assumptions of the LGB movement, then what exactly is it *for*?

Unfortunately, the answer to that question will have to wait. First we need to understand a little more of how queer theorists understand their movement. And for that, we turn to a book called *Saint Foucault*, written by queer theorist David Halperin. Michel Foucault is considered one of the pioneers of the queer movement, and in the book Saint Foucault, David Halperin relates how Foucault's thinking became a core element of the queer theory toolset.

To understand why Halperin praises Foucault so highly, we need to read Halperin's description of queerness:

> ...a new kind of sexual identity, one characterized by its lack of a clear definitional content. The homosexual subject can now claim an identity without an essence.
>
> ...defined wholly relationally, by its distance to and difference from the normative.
>
> (Homo)sexual identity can now be constituted not substantively but oppositionally, not by what it is but by where it is and how it operates. Those who knowingly occupy such a marginal location, who assume a de-essentialized identity that is purely positional in

---

7   Weikart, "Marx, Engels, and the Abolition of the Family."

character, are properly speaking not gay but queer.[8]

Okay- if you feel confused by what was just said, that is a normal response. But let's translate elements of Halperin's definition, one by one:

...a new kind of sexual identity, one characterized by its lack of a clear definitional content. The homosexual subject can now claim an identity without an essence. Here Halperin is saying that the word queer lacks an essential definition. In other words, a gay-identifying individual might say that his sexual orientation is part of his essence as a human being, and this is the view held by Fred Sargeant and others. But queer theory says the opposite, that everything about a person is socially constructed. So, queer is a way of claiming a new identity that is not tied to anything that one might consider essential, like biological sex or sexual orientation.

...defined wholly relationally, by its distance to and difference from the normative. This means that to know how queer something is, you have to see how strongly it differs from normal. That is the only way to assess the "queerness" of anything.

...constituted not substantively but oppositionally... means that queerness is only about opposition to norms. Nothing else.

Halperin offers an honest appraisal of the problems with the idea of queer, a word to convey identity, but without any specific definition other than opposition to norms. In our chapter 3 discussion of intersectionality, we noted that intersectional thinking creates incentives for people to opt into "marginalized" identities, and the

---

8   Halperin, *Saint Foucault: Towards a Gay Hagiography*. p.61

label "queer" provides an easy way to do that. Halperin acknowledges this:

> Lesbians and gay men can now look forward to a new round of condescension and dismissal at the hands of the trendy and glamorously unspecified sexual outlaws who call themselves "queer" and who can claim the radical chic attached to a sexually transgressive identity without, of course, having to do anything icky with their bodies in order to earn it. There is nothing enviable about the lot of lesbians and gay men who wind up living in the sort of queer world where, as a friend of mine reports about a certain New England women's college, all the women who are sleeping with men identify themselves as lesbians and all the women who are sleeping with women identify themselves as bisexuals.[9]

To illustrate how queer theory makes everything incoherent, consider an article on the website wellandgood.com, entitled "Can Straight People Call Themselves Queer Without Being Appropriative? It's Complicated" The author, Gabrielle Kassel, answers the question of the title: "Plainly put, yes, someone who is straight can indeed be queer, so long as they are not cisgender or not allosexual."[10] The obvious problem, though, is that the author has just articulated a norm. And norms are outside the bounds of queer thinking. This is because norms lead to "gatekeeping," which queer theorists consider a form of oppression.

And so, many LGB rights activists who have fought for decades for LGB causes are appalled to read commentary such as the following from writer Stacey May Fowles:

---

9 Ibid.

10 Kassel, "Queer Cultural Appropriation: Can Straight Really Be Queer?"

> I also refuse to entertain the light-hearted critique that my intense attraction to gay male and queer culture is an offshoot of the fact that I'm looking to fail because "I'm not ready for a relationship." Instead, I've started to accept the fact that I love and feel comfortable with gay and queer-identified men because-wait for it-I am queer myself, and I tout the burgeoning theory of sexual fluidity as my rationale. I suppose I'm finally accepting the notion that there can indeed be straight queers and that it's more than okay for me to define myself as one.
>
> We (and yes, I'm including myself-shock! horror!) have worked hard to develop a queer identity that lives outside of merely who we go to bed with; so why can't I, a heterosexual who feels most at home in queer culture, adopt it as a result?[11]

Earlier we asked the question of what queer theory is for, and by now the answer should be clear: queer theory is for being opposed to norms. Norms are rules, guidelines, specificity, distinctions, definitions for terms, consistent shared understandings, and other things that bring coherence to our understanding of the world and how we live. Queer theory is what happens when someone develops a basic hatred of all of those things, and they express that hatred using academic jargon.

The Consequences of Queer Theory

Queer theory can seem like nothing more than a ridiculous academic framework for expressing one's emotional underdevelopment, or their oppositional defiant disorder. But in fact, queer theory has tremendous

---

11 Schimel and Labonté, *First Person Queer: Who We Are (so Far)*.

harmful consequences outside of academia, in the real world.

At the heart of queer theory is a personally-felt terror over exclusion. And what are some of the things that can cause people to feel excluded?

- To say that a sexual attraction or behavior is not normal
- To say that sex and gender are synonymous and that they exist in binary, male and female
- To say that men and women should have their own spaces and unique roles in society
- To say that a sexual fetish is abnormal or disgusting
- To say that there is a form of family that represents the ideal

…and more. To say that anything at all is normal, is to exclude. This is a reality of life, that cannot be avoided.

Michel Foucault viewed norms and everything else in terms of power. His philosophy around discourse and power arose from his personal life; he was consumed with sexual perversion, which is reflected in his attempts to associate norms with exercise of power. In his article "The Perversions of Michel Foucault," Roger Kimball reviews James Miller's biography of Foucault and concludes,

> Foucault once described his writing as a "labyrinth." He was right. The question is, why should we wish to enter it? It may be the case that, as Miller insists, Foucault's writing expresses "a powerful desire to realize a certain form of life." But is it a desirable form of life? Foucault's personal perversions involved him in private tragedy. The celebration of his intellectual perversions by academics continues to be a public scandal. The career of this "representative man" of the twentieth century really represents one of the biggest con jobs in recent

intellectual history.[12]

After a debate with Michel Foucault in 1971, progressive activist Noam Chomsky said of Foucault, "He struck me as completely amoral. I'd never met anyone who was so totally amoral."[13]

In an effort to eliminate the possibility of someone – even someone "totally amoral" – feeling excluded, queer theory simply attempts to destroy (or "deconstruct") any and all of the ways of thinking that might result in someone's sense of exclusion. This means that nothing can be labeled good or bad, normal or abnormal, or any other label that implies any kind of evaluation.

In 2020 I wrote an article for Public Square Magazine called "And Not One Soul Shall Feel Excluded,"[14] where the title is a play on the premortal claim of Satan that "not one soul shall be lost." I chose that title to convey that there is a lie in the idea that no one should ever feel excluded. It is a delusional goal, and striving for that goal leads to very destructive decision-making.

In an effort to be inclusive, the queer movement has become intertwined with gender theory, obliterating any notions that there is any basis for perceiving real differences in biological sex. Activists have successfully pushed for the allowance of biological males in women's sports, excluding women from participation, earnings, and scholarships. This is one of the ways that the queer movement has destroyed not just the LGB movement, but also the feminist movement, by emotionally extorting

---

12 Kimball, "The Perversions of M. Foucault | The New Criterion."

13 Miller, *The Passion of Michel Foucault*. p.201

14 Ellsworth, "And Not One Soul Shall Feel Excluded."

women – in the name of inclusion – to exclude and remove other women from competitive opportunities.[15] The queer movement has also embraced a concept called "age queer,"[16] where people can identify as an age other than their chronological years since birth. For just one example, in 2023, this led to a 50-year-old biological male entering a swimming competition against teenage girls, including sharing their locker room.[17]

On a recent episode of the Blocked and Reported podcast, progressive commentator Ana Kasparian detailed the immense backlash she faced after insisting on being called a woman, instead of gender theory-inspired "inclusive" terms like "birthing person" or "person with a uterus."[18] Kasparian's story illustrates that it is not possible to make everyone feel included. Queer theory and gender theory tend to exclude people who have a basic psychological orientation toward honesty and reality.

In 2019, feminist commentator Dr. Em Pankhurst published a series of articles that revealed a deeper evil in queer theory: the tendency for queer theorists to legitimize pedophilia. She noted of Michel Foucault that

> In 1977 Foucault signed a petition to the French Parliament arguing for the abolition of all legislation regarding the age of consent, the effective legalisation of paedophilia. In 1978 Foucault participated in a radio broadcast which once again argued that age of consent legislation should be abolished and that children's

---

15 "578+ Male* Victories in Female Sports."

16 Backer, "Age Queer."

17 Koenig, "50-Year-Old Transgender Woman Shared Pool, Locker Room with Young Girls at Race."

18 Herzog, "Episode 213."

sexuality and supposed desire for sex with adults should be acknowledged.[19]

Pankhurst noted of queer theorist Gayle Rubin,

> Rubin celebrated that "Sexualities keep marching out of the Diagnostic and Statistical Manual and on to the pages of social history. At present, several other groups are trying to emulate the successes of homosexuals. Bisexuals, sadomasochists, individuals who prefer cross-generational encounters, transsexuals, and transvestites are all in various states of community formation and identity acquisition."
>
> …Rubin continues to bemoan that "the law is especially ferocious in maintaining the boundary between childhood 'innocence' and 'adult' sexuality." One would have thought this was a positive thing, well not in queer theory.[20]

There are more examples that can be cited, but I am reminded of Mormon's statement describing the downfall of his people, that "…behold, I, Mormon, do not desire to harrow up the souls of men in casting before them such an awful scene…" (Mormon 5:8)

In the name of inclusivity, queer and gender theory invite human beings into depths of depravity that are too vast to be described here. Entire books could be written on trans ideology alone- the lies at the heart of it, and the trails of human wreckage it leaves in its wake. All of these are fruits of the Marxist worldview, springing from various branches over decades through the minds of neo-Marxist intellectuals.

---

19 Pankhurst, "The Trojan Unicorn Part 1."

20 Pankhurst, "The Trojan Unicorn Part 2."

A Gospel View of Gender and Queer Theory

There is no modern prophetic statement more hotly contested and also more resoundingly, decisively vindicated in our observable world, than the 1995 Proclamation on the Family. The proclamation's clear teachings on gender and marriage, and its clear doctrinal statements about procreation and family life, are beacons of clarity in a world that is consumed with the chaos invited by critical theory. In 1995, few Latter-day Saints could have imagined how prophetic the proclamation would turn out to be in our day.

One of the strongest differentiators between our doctrines and the neo-Marxist fields of queer theory and gender theory has to do with identity. The Family Proclamation declares the following:

> *All human beings—male and female—are created in the image of God. Each is a beloved spirit son or daughter of heavenly parents, and, as such, each has a divine nature and destiny. Gender is an essential characteristic of individual premortal, mortal, and eternal identity and purpose.*[21]

This paragraph in the proclamation states with clarity the nature of identity: we are spirit children of heavenly parents, male and female, and we existed as such long before our present experiences in mortality (including our sexual attractions, our perceptions around gender, and other dimensions of our mortal life).

By contrast, queer and gender theory assert that *our present experiences are identity*. Our desires, our frustrations, our perceptions, our feelings, our personality traits, or even something like a sexual fetish- any and all of

---

21 The Church of Jesus Christ of Latter-day Saints, "The Family Proclamation."

these are the basis of identity. These things are *who we are, our authentic selves*. This notion of identity is incompatible with the gospel.

The political activism arising from queer theory and gender theory also contains the assumptions of intersectionality, where the further from norms a person goes, the more "marginalized" they are, and therefore the more they are entitled to "empathy" and privileges in society. Now, recall in our chapter 3 discussion of intersectionality, where we discussed the twisted incentives of intersectional thinking, leading to false claims of marginalized racial identity. The same phenomenon is evident in the world of queer. We mentioned earlier the claiming of queer identity among straight people, but that is only one example.

A recent study in the Archives of Sexual Behavior called "Intersex Pretenders" explored fabrications in people's declarations that they have an intersex condition. In their speculations over the motives for this behavior, the study authors offered that "Some appear, similarly to persons with factitious disorder, to be seeking attention and/or the role of a sick, disadvantaged, or victimized person."[22]

A gospel-based identity in our relationship to heavenly parents leads us to need less and less from the world. This means less affirmation, attention, validation, and other things that the intersectional mind can never get enough of. In a shocking online video in 2020, lesbian commentator Arielle Scarcella made a public break from the LGBTQ+ movement, where she lamented,

> Never in my life have I been more cancelled, tortured,

---

22 Cadet, "Intersex Pretenders."

tormented, harassed, than by members of my own community. Never have I witnessed literal mentally-ill individuals who are latching themselves onto the LGBT community without actually being LGBT, for the sake of oppression points, validation, and sympathy.[23]

What Scarcella described was the natural outcome of queer theory, where people derive their sense of worth from the affirmation and attention of others. Without a core sense of identity in God, this is just one of the bottomless psychological pits where human beings tend to go in desperation for a sense of meaning and significance.

And the institutions of capitalism are all too eager to accommodate people in their embrace of queer and gender theory. Queer-themed corporate advertising signals to the world that profit-focused enterprises are bucking the hegemony of sexual norms, and the medical and pharmaceutical industries find ways to profit from gender confusion. As feminist activist Kara Dansky noted in a recent book,

> In January 2022, Stanford University published a study by Turban called "Access to Gender-Affirming Hormones During Adolescence and Mental Health Outcomes Among Transgender Adults." That study was funded in large part by the companies Arbor Pharmaceuticals and Pfizer, both of which produce hormones that are used in "gender-affirmation care."[24]

Here again, capitalist systems rise to the challenge: they provide goods and services that become necessitated by the

---

23 Arielle Scarcella, *I'm A Lesbian Woman & I'm Leaving The INSANE "Progressive" Left.*

24 Dansky, *The Reckoning: How the Democrats and the Left Betrayed Women and Girls.*

Marxist worldview and the notions of identity that arise in branches of Marxist thinking. By contrast, the value of an identity in God is not something that we purchase by meeting a price in a market of buyers and sellers. The price of identity in God was expressed beautifully in the Book of Mormon, where the father of King Lamoni said "…if thou art God, wilt thou make thyself known unto me, and *I will give away all my sins to know thee…*" (Alma 22:18).

With all of this in mind, one of the interesting developments that queer theory has brought about has been the refutation of some basic arguments long promoted by the LGB movement, regarding the essential and permanent nature of sexual attractions. This is an area where, surprisingly, queer theorists to some extent have science on their side.

In recent years it has been demonstrated in numerous studies that sexual attraction is fluid, and in many cases can change.[25] This has long been a claim of queer theorists, and they have been proven right.

I would never claim that there has ever been any amount of real alignment between prophets and queer theorists. But what is very clear is the fact that prophets' past stances of skepticism toward the claims of both the LGB movement and also queer and gender theorists have been clearly validated over time.

A final interesting point of discussion in the area of restoration doctrine versus queer and gender theory has to do with our belief in heavenly parents that are gendered male and female. It is very common for Latter-day Saint

---

25 For additional resources, see https://nauvooneighbor.org/gospel-grounded-understanding-of-and-ministry-to-sexual-minorities/

women in particular to embrace our doctrine of a heavenly mother and yearn to know more of her.

But Latter-day Saints and former church members who embrace queer theory find themselves facing an irreconcilable conflict between a belief in a heavenly mother and a belief in their newly-adopted theories. This was well illustrated in a Sunstone presentation from 2015, where panelists offered a presentation called "Why I Don't Need Heavenly Mother." One of the panelists explained queer theory's problem as follows:

> ...there are a multiplicity of sexes and genders and sex-gender pairings in mortality, and this implies a need for a divine archetype of each one. If there is a heterosexual god couple, why can't there be a gay or lesbian god couple, or a polyamorous couple, or an intersex god? But why stop there?[26]

The massive problems in logic and worldview that we find in this short statement alone, could fill an entire book. But there are a couple of things that we can understand, and the first is that venues like Sunstone have fully adopted Marx's view that "The criticism of religion disillusions man, so that he will think, act, and fashion his reality like a man who has discarded his illusions and regained his senses, so that he will move around himself as his own true Sun."[27] In presentations like the Sunstone panel quoted above, people tend to combine criticism of religion with a lot of discussion about themselves. I doubt if many of them would consider themselves Marxists in the classical sense

---

26 Sunstone, "Why I Don't Need Heavenly Mother."

27 Marx, "A Contribution to the Critique of Hegel's Philosophy of Right 1844."

of economically-focused social theory, but they certainly share the Marxist worldview as it pertains to religion.

Where these commentators fail on a basic level, is in their epistemology. Latter-day Saints who hold restoration convictions about the nature of God, do so because they give primacy to witness testimony as a source of truth. We believe specific things about God because we have seen and experienced specific things about God. Without direct experience, people make gods out of their thoughts, feelings, desires, and theories. It's a Western consumerist approach to religion that assumes, as many corporations profess, that "the customer is always right."

The conclusions of the sunstone panel are a product of their assumptions, which are based in queer theory. And if queer theory is an accurate guide to reality, or if we take the queer theorist view that questions around reality do not matter anyway, then of course there is no basis for a belief in a heavenly mother because femininity and motherhood are just earthly concepts that we socially construct, instead of eternal realities apart from us, that we discover.

Marx taught that "Man makes religion," and queer theorists have fully adopted that view, seeing God and doctrine as entirely products of human creativity. Queer theorists encountering the Church of Jesus Christ of Latter-day Saints will only ever find frustration in our epistemology, which is primarily based upon direct experience of God that we find confirmed in the testimony of scripture.

Chapter 6

The Historical Fruits of Marxism

Marx was a man with a particular vision of how the history of the world would go over time. He envisioned stages of world history that would culminate in a collapse of capitalism, and that there would be an ushering in of a new way of living where there would not be alienation or economic classes. In the mind of Marx and those who accepted his vision, this was simply the way that history would go. It was inevitable; it was destined to happen.

In the 1956 book *When Prophecy Fails*, the authors discussed what happens when a charismatic leader predicts the end of the world, and then the end of the world does not happen as predicted. Intuitively we might imagine that people would abandon this leader, but in reality, often they do not. People in these situations experience *cognitive dissonance*, which is where our understanding of the world is challenged by our observed reality. Many followers find creative ways to resolve their cognitive dissonance, and they continue their devotion to the leader.[1]

When we consider the movements that arose from the theories of Karl Marx, it is important to understand that each of those movements had some degree of cognitive dissonance toward Marx's ideas, and some Marxist movements produced their own new streams of cognitive dissonance among Marxists. We learned in Chapter 2 that Antonio Gramsci developed his notion of cultural hegemony and the Frankfurt School expanded it, more or less as a response to cognitive dissonance over the fact that capitalism was doing very well and was producing happy people, contrary to the Marxist vision of the future.

Gramsci's cognitive dissonance began in his observation of Russia, where Marxist Vladimir Lenin spearheaded a revolution. Gramsci initially thought of the Russian experience as an ideal model for what could happen everywhere, but then noticed that the Russians had diverged strongly from Marx's vision. Gramsci concluded, though, that Russia's revolution had been Marxist in a deeper way, maybe even more Marxist than Marx himself:

> The Bolsheviks renounce Karl Marx and they assert, through their clear statement of action, through what they have achieved, that the laws of historical materialism are not as set in stone, as one may think, or one may have thought previously.
>
> Yet, there is still a certain amount of inevitability to these events, and if the Bolsheviks reject some of that which is affirmed in Capital, they do not reject its inherent, invigorating idea. They are not 'Marxists', that's what it comes down to: they have not used the

---

[1] Festinger, Riecken, and Schachter, *When Prophecy Fails*

Master's works to draw up a superficial interpretation, dictatorial statements which cannot be disputed. They live out Marxist thought, the one which will never die; the continuation of idealist Italian and German thought, and that in Marx had been corrupted by the emptiness of positivism and naturalism.[2]

In other words, Gramsci saw Russia diverging from Marx's vision, but he resolved his cognitive dissonance by saying that the Russians were living a form of Marxist thought that was even more pure than the "corrupted" thinking of Karl Marx!

Russia's Marxist Authoritarianism

In Russia, Vladimir Lenin modeled to the world a vision of what Marx called the "dictatorship of the proletariat," which in practice meant that Russia was to become a violently oppressive totalitarian state. In Lenin's words, "First throw off the yoke of money, the power of capital, abolish private property, then the slow growth of 'conscientiousness' on this new basis."[3] The revolution would eliminate the systems that had perpetuated alienation and inequities, and that process would be one of horror and cruelty to bring about a new Marxist consciousness.

During the time of Lenin, Russia at least tried to maintain some semblance of adherence to Marx's vision. But with the death of Lenin and the rise of Josef Stalin, Russia made its full transformation into a totalitarian regime focused on the vision of a psychopathic dictator.

---

2   Gramsci, "The Revolution Against Capital."

3   Lenin, "The Dictatorship Of The Proletariat."

Notably, one of the victims of Stalin's horrors was the Marxist scholar David Riazanov, whom many had regarded as the most intelligent figure in the Russian revolution. Riazanov was executed during Stalin's purges in 1938. According to the Marxist publication Jacobin, "Riazanov's execution sounded the death knell for serious engagement with the work of Marx within the borders of a state that had been founded in his name."[4]

Josef Stalin regarded himself as a Marxist, though his Marxist critics view him as, at best, a Marxist who lost his way. Marxism seems to have been mostly a vehicle for Stalin to acquire power and unleash his cruel depravity upon the world. But Stalin came to epitomize what has now become a standard approach to Marxist activism: the revision of history. After Stalin rose to power, he undertook a rewriting of Russian history. This attempt to create an imaginary past is a common Marxist impulse.

In Marxist movements, the past, present and future must all be understood together as part of a larger flow of history toward a worldwide utopian ideal, and this involves recasting people, groups, and even nations of the past as heroes or villains depending on whether or not they advance the narrative. In Marxist revisionist history of colonialism, for example, colonized peoples are depicted as having lived in a state of advanced, enlightened purity until exploitative Westerners arrived at their borders.

In his book *Colonialism: A Reckoning*, Nigel Biggar explores these storytelling tendencies in depth, and how hard it has become to engage in this revisionist historiography in the present day with modern online tools for fact checking. It has become hard for West African

---

4   Varela, "David Riazanov, a Revolutionary Scholar of Marxism."

countries to support reparations for slavery, for example, as it has become impossible to deny that their populations were greatly complicit in the slave trade.[5]

A need for the past to become something other than what it really was, is essential to Marxist historiography. In this, Stalin was manifesting the larger problem of the Marxist worldview and its orientation away from reality.

In one horrible sense, however, Stalin did have a very clear picture of reality. He understood that Lenin's notion of widespread economic transformation first, was impossible to achieve without massive amounts of suffering and bloodshed. But rather than pause and reflect on what that might indicate about the human viability of communism, Stalin disregarded the cost in human life and pressed forward. He allowed his Marxist vision to morph into something like a nationalist communism, and his policies turned Russia into a frightening totalitarian police state where the proletariat became victims of state-sanctioned murder by the millions.

Marxism in Maoist China

As recently as 1967, during the horrors of the Cultural revolution in China, Marxist dictator Mao Tse-Tung was being praised by communists as "Comrade Mao Tse-Tung, the greatest Marxist-Leninist alive."[6] 1967 was a full five years after Mao's Great Leap Forward, a centrally-planned push for industrialization that resulted in the deaths of tens of millions of Chinese peasants.

---

5   Biggar, *Colonialism: A Moral Reckoning.* p.342

6   Sanmugathasan, "Mao Tse-Tung's Contribution to Marxism-Leninism."

Mao Tse-Tung saw himself as a Chinese participant in the legacy of Lenin in Russia, referring to Lenin's thinking constantly in his speeches. Mao was deeply versed in Marxist theory, but like Lenin, Mao viewed revolution and active conflict as the means for bringing about the ideal future society envisioned by Marx. In the mind of Mao, it was not possible to understand the movement unless and until one was actively participating in it:

> If you want knowledge, you must take part in the practice of changing reality. If you want to know the taste of a pear, you must change the pear by eating it yourself. If you want to know the structure and properties of the atom, you must make physical and chemical experiments to change the state of the atom. If you want to know the theory and methods of revolution, you must take part in revolution.[7]

Mao's Marxist revolution was a conflict against Chinese nationalist and imperialist forces, and when he assumed power in 1949, he undertook to transform all of Chinese society to reflect his Marxist vision. Like Stalin, Mao created a cult of personality from which he dispensed "revolutionary" directives to his followers. But Maoist Marxism had some unique elements to it that have become integral to the modern Marxist worldview, and one of the most impactful is the *external locus of control*. To help understand what that phrase means, let's first see how it was manifest in Mao's Marxist vision for China.

In Mao's cultural revolution, he deployed a concept called the "four olds": old ideas, old culture, old customs, and old habits. He led his followers to understand that the destruction of these "four olds" was a new precursor

---

7   Mao Tse-Tung, "ON PRACTICE."

The Historical Fruits of Marxism

to bringing the revolution to fruition. In this, Maoism shared Gramsci's and the Frankfurt School's sense of the importance of culture and other aspects of the superstructure. But when Mao's messaging around the four olds reached the masses, the effect was not to remove the power of culture; rather, culture became an obsession. The four olds dominated Chinese thinking to a greater degree than ever before.

Chinese writer Jung Chang recalled,

> To fill us with hatred for class enemies, the schools started regular sessions of "recalling bitterness and reflecting on happiness," at which older people would tell us about the miseries of pre-Communist China. Our generation had been born "under the red flag" in new China, and had no idea what life was like under the Kuomintang. Lei Feng had, we were taught, which was why he could hate the class enemies so deeply and love Chairman Mao with all his heart. When he was seven, his mother was supposed to have hanged herself after being raped by a landlord. Workers and peasants came to give talks at our school: we heard of childhoods dominated by starvation, freezing winters with no shoes, and premature, painful deaths. They told us how boundlessly grateful they were to Chairman Mao for saving their lives and giving them food and clothing. One speaker was a member of an ethnic group called the Yi, who had a system of slavery until the late 1950s. He had been a slave and showed us scars from appalling beatings under his previous masters. Every time the speakers described the hardships they had endured the packed hall was shaken by sobs.[8]

---

8   Chang, *Wild Swans: Three Daughters of China*. pp. 316-317

Whereas Stalin's approach to history had attempted to disappear from national memory some of the people and narratives of the Russian past, Mao created in Chinese society a burning fixation on the past that led to a wave of harassment, torture, and murder. There emerged a revolutionary practice called the *struggle session*, where a person accused of being against the revolution, or part of the capitalist past, would be publicly harassed and tortured, often to death.

Whether intended or not, the message of the cultural revolution was that *the past has unlimited power over the present*. People's sins of the past, whether real or imagined, determine our ability to function well in the here and now. This is what psychologists refer to as external locus of control, the idea that our ability to be happy and well in the world exists outside of ourselves, in "powerful others." In Mao's vision, the "powerful others" preventing the well-being of all Chinese were figures of the past who had participated in capitalist systems of oppression.

And what were the results of this view? In China, the Cultural Revolution is estimated to have killed up to 2 million people, with many more beaten and tortured. Families were broken up by the state and children were sent away from their parents for "reeducation" in rural life. Chinese society has never fully recovered from the horrors of Maoist Marxism.

Marxism in Cambodia

In 2014, a UN court secured convictions for crimes against humanity against leaders of the Khmer Rouge, the communist government that ruled Cambodia from 1975-1979. Later in 2016, one of the Khmer Rouge leaders attempted to gain an appeal for his life sentence. Khieu Samphan tried to sway the court by expressing his intentions as one of the leaders in that movement: "What I want to say today and what I want my countrymen to hear is that as an intellectual I have never wanted anything other than social justice for my country."[9]

The Khmer Rouge was supported and funded by the Chinese Communist Party, and they imitated Mao Tse-Tung's Great Leap Forward, with similar results. The USC Shoah Foundation offers a summary of the short rule of the Khmer Rouge:

> The Khmer Rouge held power in Cambodia for just under 45 months (April 1975-January 1979) and left 1.6–3 million Cambodian civilians dead through starvation, torture, execution, medical experiments, untreated diseases, forced marches, forced labor, and other forms of violence. However, even after 1979, the Khmer Rouge remained active in remote regions of the country; thus, fatalities may be higher than documented.
>
> ...The Khmer Rouge based their policies on the idea that citizens of Cambodia had become corrupted by outside influences, especially Vietnam and the capitalist West. The Khmer Rouge referred to people who supported their vision as "pure people," and persecuted anyone they deemed "impure." Within days of taking power, the regime killed thousands of military personnel and forcibly moved millions of people out of cities, killing anyone who refused or was too slow. They forced citizens into what they called reeducation schools, which were essentially places of state propaganda.
>
> The regime forced families to live communally with

---

9 "Top Khmer Rouge Leader Tells Court He Fought for 'Social Justice.'"

other people, in order to destroy the family structure. The Khmer Rouge targeted ethnic minorities, especially Chinese, Vietnamese, and Muslim Cham, of whom an estimated 80% were killed. In addition, anyone who was believed to be an intellectual was killed: doctors, lawyers, teachers, even people who wore glasses or knew a foreign language became targets.[10]

The communist ideology of the Khmer Rouge shared with Stalinism a nationalistic focus, but in terms of tactics, it was Maoist. But instead of moving in stages, the Khmer Rouge attempted to rapidly, all at once, transform the entirety of Cambodian society. In their words,

> We have leaped over the neocolonial, semi-feudalist society of the American imperialists, the feudalists and capitalists of every nation, and have achieved a socialist society straight away … [In China] a long period of time was required … [North Korea] needed fourteen years to make the transition. North Vietnam did the same. As for us, we have a different character from them. We are faster than they are.[11]

In the name of social justice, the Khmer Rouge moved quickly to implement the entirety of what they understood to be Marx's vision of an ideal society. In the process, they wiped out around a quarter of Cambodia's population.

Fascism: the Yang to the Marxist Yin

Fascism is often considered to be antithetical to Marxism, and in a sense this is true. But the basic elements of the fascist and Marxist worldviews are very similar.

---

10 USC Shoah Foundation, "Cambodian Genocide."

11 Himel, "Khmer Rouge Irrigation Development in Cambodia."

The Historical Fruits of Marxism

When we observe fighting between fascist and Marxist movements in society, these fights are not between opposites; they are between ideologies that are so close together in so many ways that their mutual hostility resembles an ugly sibling rivalry.

In his book Liberal Fascism, Jonah Golberg explains:

> ...fascism, properly understood, is not a phenomenon of the right at all. Instead, it is, and always has been, a phenomenon of the left. This fact—an inconvenient truth if there ever was one—is obscured in our time by the equally mistaken belief that fascism and communism are opposites. In reality, they are closely related, historical competitors for the same constituents, seeking to dominate and control the same social space.[12]

Reflecting on Goldberg's claim, recall that earlier in this book, we set forth key components of the Marxist worldview. The foundational component is the idea that there exists an ideal society, and it is possible to create that society apart from God. Fascism fully shares this basic assumption.

The fundamental difference between Marxism and fascism is that Marxism sees the ideal society emerging through the abolition of property and class differences, whereas fascism sees the ideal society emerging through unity of blood and soil, ethnic and national identity. But as we saw in the example of the Khmer Rouge, sometimes these two visions can merge into one.

Also with the Khmer Rouge, we witnessed a merging of Marxist and fascist notions of *purity*. Since the time of Lenin, every Marxist knows that Marx's vision of historical

---

12 Goldberg, *Liberal Fascism: The Secret History of the Left from Mussolini to the Politics of Meaning.* p.7

progression will never happen organically, the way Marx envisioned. Marx's understanding of history simply failed to emerge in reality. For this reason, Marxist movements became activist revolutionary movements, intending to forcibly bring about the world that Marx envisioned.

The problem is that Marx's vision of the future only works if everyone is fully committed to it, heart and mind. Marxists speak of a fundamentally new universal human consciousness that needs to emerge in order for class differences to disappear, but what if some people do not desire this new consciousness? This is the problem that Marxist violence has long tried in vain to solve. Whereas fascists define purity in terms of race and nationality, Marxists define purity in ideological terms. In the Marxist worldview, *thinking wrong things* is the gravest of sins because wrong thinking among human beings is what prevents the world from achieving its great transformation into a post-capitalist utopia.

These opposing notions of purity – purity of thought and purity of nationality – were merged together under the Khmer Rouge's regime of nationalist communism in Cambodia.

In another example that illustrates the similarities in these ideologies, consider that in 2022, Italy elected prime minister Giorgia Meloni, who was labeled "far-right" and "fascist" by numerous commentators on the left. But it's interesting to examine the actual concerns that animate her political activity. In a March 2019 speech to the World Congress of Families, Meloni said the following:

> Why is the family an enemy? Why is the family so scary? There is a unique answer to all these questions: because it defines who we are, and because it is our identity. Why is everything that defines us at this time an enemy to

> those who would like us to no longer have an identity and simply be slaves, perfect consumers?
>
> So they attack national identity.
>
> They attack religious identity.
>
> They attack [binary gender].
>
> They attack family identity.
>
> I must not be able to call myself Italian, Christian, woman, mother. No! I must be citizen X, gender X, parent 1, parent 2. I must be a number, because when I am just a number, when I have no identity, when I have no roots, then I will be the perfect slave at the mercy of big financial speculators. The perfect consumer![13]

What Meloni is describing here is a set of powerful and impersonal capitalist forces that are causing people to feel alienated. But unlike the Marxist view that we become alienated from our personal essence when we give our labor to property owners, this other view of alienation defines alienation in terms of removal of national, family, and other forms of identity.

Meloni is not a fascist. And the Marxist-leaning critics who label her one are perhaps revealing more about themselves than they intend to. It's interesting that with a few tweaks of wording – for example, replacing "family" with "marginalized identity," and replacing the other identity descriptors with intersectional terms – this part of her speech could come to resemble a neo-Marxist rallying cry against capitalist oppression and cultural hegemony. To a neo-Marxist, Meloni is using the right formula, only with the wrong variables.

---

13   YouTube, "Full Speech of Giorgia Meloni at WCF Verona 2019."

When we hear political messaging that fascists hate Marxists and vice-versa, that's only true in a limited sense. In a twisted way, political opponents like Fascists and Marxists actually come to love each other, because lacking an identity in God, both of these groups need a reason to get up in the morning and face life. Their relationship with each other is symbiotic. They need an animating cause for their existence, something to give their lives meaning and make them feel righteous. They derive energy and life force from each other. They are each other's oppositional identity. They simply would not know what to do without each other.

The historical fruits of Marxism are the exchange of capitalist oppression for other, different forms of oppression: untold numbers of people mass murdered under Marxist regimes, and ideological oppression among regimes that attempted to coerce a new Marxist consciousness into everyone they possibly could. This coercion is described well by Paul Kengor:

> No other political ideology has produced as much wretched poverty, rank repression, and sheer violence. In country after country, implemented in varying forms across wide-ranging nationalities, traditions, backgrounds, faiths, and ethnicities, communism coldly and consistently violated the full sweep of most basic human rights, from property to press, from speech to assembly, from conscience to religion. So restrictive was communism in the twentieth century that its implementers routinely refused to allow citizens the right to exit (that is, escape) the destructive systems imposed within their borders. In some cases, they erected walls to herd and fence in the "masses" they claimed to champion.
>
> That bears repeating: so restrictive was communism

that its advocates had to build walls—poured with cement, topped with barbed wire, patrolled 24/7 by secret police with automatic weapons turned on their own citizenry—to keep their people from fleeing.[14]

In addition to the horrors of Marxist violent oppression, another fruit of Marxism – though an inadvertent one – has been the development of a fascist reaction in many parts of the world. As new branches of Marxist thinking continue to gain traction in many places, we should expect to see this dynamic of Marxism feeding and developing its own mirror-image in the form of fascist movements that emerge to counter its influence.

A Note on Luxury Beliefs

In his memoir *Troubled*, writer Rob Henderson developed the concept of *luxury beliefs*. These are beliefs that are professed among upper-class people, and professing these beliefs serves to maintain and enhance social status. But living these beliefs is very costly, and the costs of luxury beliefs among the upper class are paid by the lower classes.

Henderson's memoir is a difficult story of his journey through youth with experiences of family abandonment, abuse, addiction, and movement through the foster care system. And through his tragic upbringing has emerged one of his deepest convictions, the value of a warm, stable, and loving family life.

The logic of luxury beliefs applies very powerfully to questions of family. Many neo-Marxists who profess

---

14 Kengor, *The Devil and Karl Marx: Communism's Long March of Death, Deception, and Infiltration*. (Kindle location 141)

a belief in queer theory, for example, are people raising children in the traditional nuclear family structure where children know the loving presence of their father and their mother. Their children are spared the deep pain and confusion of being conceived to be raised intentionally without their birth mother or father, or the pain and confusion of watching their father conclude he is now a woman, or other traumatic experiences that queer and gender theory insist are somehow not to be regarded as traumatic. Queer and gender theorists delude themselves and others by dismissing the real trauma of broken family bonds as "socially constructed," but that claim will never fool people like Rob Henderson who live the actual experience.

A wealthy, upper-class family that professes a belief in queer and gender theory might have a daughter playing competitive sports, but they are unlikely to be financially impacted by a biological male identifying as female and then depriving their daughter of scholarship money. It is very easy to profess these beliefs when a couple has nothing personal at stake, when the real negative consequences of their beliefs are felt only by people further down the socioeconomic ladder.

The same goes for beliefs that emerge in other neo-Marxist contexts; for example, earlier in this book we discussed the "defund the police" movement, which devastated so many communities of lower-income people of color before higher-class politicians sensed political consequences of that luxury belief and reversed their policy positions.

Neo-Marxism tends to produce these luxury beliefs that are theoretically valid in the minds of elites, but devastate people in lower classes where the beliefs are actually experienced in real life as public policy. This also happens to be true of classical Marxism that is less focused on cultural concerns and is more narrowly focused on questions of capital and economics.

During historical periods where the Marxist vision has been attempted in various parts of the world, there have always been cheerleaders in elite Western circles who have professed support for these movements that have inflicted untold suffering upon the poor.

A simple way of assessing whether a belief is sincerely held as a result of honest truth-seeking, or whether it is just a luxury belief held to enhance one's social status, is the question:

Would you like to see this belief actually implemented in your life and the lives of your children?

The honest answer for many upper-class people who profess neo-Marxist beliefs is, no. And the discrepancy between what people profess to believe is best for society, versus what they actually desire for themselves and their loved ones, is a gap of dishonesty that indicates a luxury belief.

Part 4
The Church and Marxism

Chapter 7

Marxism and Deconversion

The first thing to understand about Marxism and the church is that Marxism is incompatible with the restored gospel. We noted in our chapter on Critical Race Theory that there is a constant tendency for people who adopt the Marxist worldview to undergo a shift in perspective, where they begin to evaluate the church and the restored gospel through lenses of Marxism, instead of evaluating Marxism through the lenses of gospel principles.

In the Book of Mormon, we read in Jacob 5 an allegory of the gospel and how it is manifest among God's children throughout history. In that allegory, we read of *grafting*, the severing of branches of one tree in order to attach them to another tree. Grafting can be done to increase the health of a tree or help it to bear a different kind of fruit.

In the allegory, there are references to corrupted branches that bring forth wild fruit (v30-32), and this is an important passage for understanding the impact that the Marxist worldview has on faith.

Among the fruits of the restored gospel, we find primary fruits of love of God and neighbor; the gifts of the spirit; connection to a caring community; communion with God; and prophetic leadership.

When the branches of Marxism are grafted onto any system, that system begins to produce the fruits of Marxism, which are conflict and tyranny and horror. This is why as long as we have prophetic leadership in the church, and a core group of church members who can discern between the fruits of the restored gospel and the fruits of rival belief systems, the branches of Marxism will always be seen as corrupted toxic branches that cannot be grafted onto the restored gospel.

This is because Marxism and the restored gospel are telling two different stories about the world in which we live. And though it may be hard for many to acknowledge, Marxism answers people's cravings for religious faith and belonging. It is considered an atheist philosophy, but in fact, Marxism replaces God with another being that becomes the new focus of worship. Repeating again the words of Marx,

> The criticism of religion disillusions man, so that he will think, act, and fashion his reality like a man who has discarded his illusions and regained his senses, so that he will move around himself as his own true Sun. Religion is only the illusory Sun which revolves around man as long as he does not revolve around himself.[1]

It is clear that Marx's vision of the ideal was for each of us to be self-centered, to revolve around ourselves. And he saw religion as being the thing that prevents us from doing that. Marx called religion the "holy form of human self-estrangement." In other words, we cannot be

---

1 Marx, "A Contribution to the Critique of Hegel's Philosophy of Right 1844."

whole, integrated beings in touch with our own essential self as long as we are religious. In Marxism, Self becomes the new god that replaces whatever previous notion of God that we learned through religion, because those two understandings of God cannot coexist in the same mind.

Let's explore other concepts that are understood differently in the Marxist worldview versus the restored gospel:

Fallenness

In the restored gospel, we understand ourselves to be living in a fallen world. Fallenness is the world's essential problem. This means that the world is chaotic and we are prone to sin, or operating in ways that do not reflect God's influence. By contrast, in Marxism, the essential problem in the world is not fallenness; in the views of Marx the great problem was social structures that produce class distinctions and alienation. In neo-Marxist thinking, the essential problem has expanded to include oppression in the form of inequities; marginalization of people's identity constructs; invalidation of people's narratives of oppression, and more.

Redemption

In the restored gospel, redemption is the reversal of fallenness. Redemption comes through faith in Christ and His atonement, and by living the law of God that we have been given. By contrast, in Marxism, there is no individual redemption. Redemption is a new future event experienced collectively by humanity all at once, and it comes through the full transformation of society to align with Marxist and neo-Marxist visions of human well-being.

Conversion

In the restored gospel, conversion is a change in our nature. It is a shift away from our natural fallen and sinful ways of thinking and feeling, toward holy and Christ-centered ways of thinking and feeling. It is the gradual replacement of our understanding of reality with God's understanding of reality. By contrast, in Marxism, conversion is the awakening to new consciousness of how society is oppressive, and how activism in the form of praxis can effect change toward Marxist notions of the social ideal.

Rituals and Sacraments

In the restored gospel, we have ordinances that demonstrate our commitment to God and His covenant path, such as the sacrament that reaffirms and renews our commitments to follow Christ. In Marxism, rituals take the form of rallies, protests, pride parades, and ideologically-motivated violence. In Maoist China, struggle sessions became a collective ritual of public sacrifice to purify society, and now in neo-Marxist praxis, public online shaming and cancel culture fulfill that same function of ritual purification. Public confessions of privilege go beyond a healthy recognition of a person's limited perspective, and become a ritual sending a signal to society that a person has arrived at the correct social consciousness. Sacraments in modern Marxism include what we commonly call "coming out," a public announcement of awareness of one's marginalized identity that is followed by affirmation and celebration of that identity by other people. Other sacraments are the celebration of violation of norms: for example, the public demonstration of sexual perversion, as seen in drag shows and pride parades.

Eschatology

Eschatology is our understanding of the end of the world, including events leading up to the end, and what happens following the end. In the restored gospel, we understand that Christ will come again and transform the world as we know it. The wicked will be removed from the earth and Christ will reign during the millennium. Souls who have passed on will be resurrected, and the millennium will culminate in a final conflict followed by judgment. In Marxist eschatology, the world will be transformed into the ideal through the overthrow of capitalist systems, but Marx was not specific as to how the world would function following this overthrow.

Community

In the restored gospel, we work toward an ideal that we call Zion, which is a community united in love of God and neighbor. Zion is described in the Book of Mormon after the visit of Christ in the Americas:

> *...the people were all converted unto the Lord, upon all the face of the land, both Nephites and Lamanites, and there were no contentions and disputations among them, and every man did deal justly one with another. And they had all things common among them; therefore there were not rich and poor, bond and free, but they were all made free, and partakers of the heavenly gift. (4 Ne 1:2-3)*

Our gospel understanding of the ideal community is described in this passage as unity and equality that come through authentic conversion to the gospel. There is no specific Marxist vision for community other than shared activism. There will never be a purely Marxist equivalent to the church, or even just an equivalent to the Tabernacle Choir on Temple Square, or any other manifestation of the ability to come together and build something significant and enduring. Ironically, whenever notable things like cities or military capabilities are built in Marxist societies, it is through processes that involve the same labor alienation that Marx decried as a central problem of capitalism.

Gather Israel, or Immanentize the Eschaton

The phrase "immanentize the eschaton" is used to describe a shift in thinking among people who lose their Christian faith. They transition from a hope grounded in Christian eschatology of the second coming and the future peaceful reign of Christ, to a present-oriented activism that does not anticipate any divine transformation of the world in the future. John Michael Greer wrote of Marxism,

> Every element of Marxist theory has an exact equivalent in Christian eschatology. Primitive communism is Eden, the invention of private property is the Fall, the stages of slavery, feudalism and capitalism are the various dispensations of sacred history, and so on, right up to the Second Coming of the proletariat, the millennial state of socialism and the final arrival of communism as the New Jerusalem descending from the heavens. Point for point, it's a rephrasing of Christian myth that replaces the transcendent dimension with forces immanent in ordinary history. Marx and his followers, in other words, immanentized the Eschaton.[2]

---

2 Greer, "Immanentizing the Eschaton."

By contrast, as Latter-day Saints, we have always had a vision that we are gathering Israel, souls that are chosen with responsibilities to serve as a model to the rest of the world of how it is possible to live and thrive in covenant relationship with God. We hold to Christian eschatology – our revealed understanding of future events like the second coming and the millennium – but we also hold a Christian activist mindset that we are to make the world a better place in the here and now.

When we speak of the fruits of the restored gospel, we can point to a number of powerfully good things that we bring to the world: a cohesive community; a prosocial belief system that produces well-adjusted adults; people who can mobilize for service and relief efforts; and more. The story of Marxist movements, on the other hand, is one after another society characterized by tragedy and horror and oppression. To lessen their cognitive dissonance, Marxists often claim that none of the attempts to implement Marx's vision have been *real Marxism*.

In this, they are sort of correct. Marx produced theories, and attempts to implement those theories in the real world always tend to run up against realities that were never accounted for in the theories. The result is that Marxist revolutionaries have ended up responding to reality in ways that were not spelled out in Marx's specific writings. The obvious problem for Marxists is the fact that it is not possible under any circumstances to achieve Marx's vision exactly as he offered it. The real world always presents vastly more variables than his theories envisioned. In any case, though, when people claim we have never seen "true Marxism" tried anywhere, that is a claim designed to protect Marx and his theories from criticism. Since Marx's ideas cannot really be tried without some divergence from, or expansion upon, Marx's thinking, in the mind of a Marxist, Marx cannot ever be shown to have been wrong.

If that sounds like a religious worldview based on absolute faith, well, it is. This is why when Latter-day Saints embrace elements of the Marxist worldview, they eventually end up having to choose between one faith or the other. The Marxist worldview cannot abide the Christian worldview. As the world-renowned African-American scholar and activist Cornel West expressed it,

> I am a non-Marxist socialist in that as a Christian, I recognize certain irreconcilable differences between Marxists of whatever sort and Christians of whatever sort....My Christian perspective—mediated by the rich traditions of the Black Church that produced and sustains me—embraces depths of despair, layers of dread...and ungrounded leaps of faith alien to the Marxist tradition.[3]

This is something many of us have observed among Latter-day Saints who "go woke," which is a term that is now commonly used to describe the embrace of neo-Marxist ways of thinking. Church members end up in constant conflict with church leaders and church doctrines, erroneously applying tools of critical theory to problems that only have solutions in the restored gospel. Eventually, these Latter-day Saints end up with very little ability to sustain church leadership, and the gifts of the Spirit gradually disappear first from their lives, and then, over time, from their memory.

Church members who embrace the Marxist worldview end up reprocessing their whole church experience, and the experiences of other people, through their new Marxist

---

3 Anderson, "Cornel West, the Public Intellectual | The New Yorker."

lenses. They end up creating new narratives of their lives, and of church history, placing people and groups into the new categories of oppressed versus oppressor; privileged versus marginalized; awakened to new critical consciousness versus stuck in a state of internalized oppression based in things like patriarchy or homophobia.

This is the deconversion from the gospel that takes place when church members convert to the totalizing worldview of Marxism.

Chapter 8

Marxism and Scripture

When we think of Marxism and scripture, there are two questions to consider: the first is the question of how Marxism treats scripture; and the second is where we see elements of Marxism described in scripture.

How Marxism Treats Scripture

Marxism views scripture in the same way it views anything else: as a means to advance the Marxist vision for the world. Scripture ceases to be understood as people's stories of how God has worked in their lives, and it becomes instead a tool of activism to dismantle whatever the reader considers to be a system of oppression. What Karl Marx said about criticism of religion bears repeating: "the criticism of religion is the prerequisite of all criticism."[1]

When a Marxist opens the scriptures, he does so with a very different agenda than the agenda held by a typical Christian believer. For the Christian believer, the

---

1   Marx, "A Contribution to the Critique of Hegel's Philosophy of Right 1844."

scriptures are a source of testimony about the reality of God. They show God's intentions for the world, and how those intentions manifest in individual people's lives. They contain a panoramic view of the world, teaching us about our past, present, and future. Most importantly, they are a conduit for personal revelation. But for the Marxist, none of these are particularly important objectives for our study of scripture. Scripture is no different from any other text. And scripture becomes valuable only to the extent that it allows us to engage in criticism of religion. When scripture is not approached in that way, it ceases to be valuable, and in the mind of a Marxist it can even be considered part of the superstructure that maintains oppression in society.

It is important to recall that when Karl Marx left home for his university studies, his new group of friends and associates included people who had begun publishing articles and books that devalued scripture. Among Marx's colleagues in the Young Hegelians, David Strauss wrote a book called *The Life of Jesus, Critically Examined*. In that book, Strauss denied the miracles documented in the New Testament and claimed that those accounts were invented by the early Christian community after the fact. Karl Marx's early mentor Bruno Bauer was constantly publishing items of anti-Christian commentary, including books that described the New Testament gospels as mostly fiction.

These are likely some of the main influences in Marx's life that led him to adopt what we call a *low view* of scripture, where scripture is considered to have little or no value in terms of being a guide to the reality of God. Marx certainly was not the originator of the low view of scripture, but he quickly embraced that view when he left home, and the low view of scripture tends to be prevalent among people with a Marxist worldview.

It is possible to use Marxism as a lens for interpreting scripture, which is common in a movement called *Liberation Theology*. The basic principles of Liberation Theology were developed among Catholic priests in South America in the mid-1900s to address challenges of poverty and inequity in society. Liberation Theology maintains that the purpose of scripture is to facilitate social justice activism, sometimes including violence. Liberation theologians use the Marxist term "praxis" to describe their social activist approach to religion, which they maintain through a Marxist interpretation of scripture.

People who adhere to Liberation Theology are correct that social activism is something that is well-founded in scripture. In Isaiah 1 we read of God's refusal to accept the people's sacrifices and devotional activities because they are not taking care of the vulnerable in society (v11-19). In Jeremiah 22, Jeremiah tells the king of Judah,

> *Shalt thou reign, because thou closest thyself in cedar? did not thy father eat and drink, and do judgment and justice, and then it was well with him?*
>
> *He judged the cause of the poor and needy; then it was well with him: was not this to know me? saith the Lord. (v15-16)*

Finally, we recall in the Book of Mormon, King Benjamin's direct linking of our standing before God with our treatment of the vulnerable in society:

> *And now, for the sake of these things which I have spoken unto you—that is, for the sake of retaining a remission of your sins from day to day, that ye may walk guiltless before God—I would that ye should impart of your substance to the poor, every man according to that which he hath, such as feeding the hungry, clothing the naked, visiting the sick and administering*

> *to their relief, both spiritually and temporally, according to their wants (Mosiah 4:26).*

For the believer, there is no question that scripture teaches that God's intention is for His chosen people to make the world a better place. The problem always comes down to the particulars of how to achieve this. If believers are not careful, our approach to social activism can leave us aligned with very destructive people and movements. For Latter-day Saints, the challenge with Liberation Theology is the same as that of broader Marxism; church members who adopt Liberation Theology as their primary faith commitment run the risk of evaluating the church against principles and priorities found in Liberation Theology, instead of the other way around.

Marxism In Scripture

Where do we see elements of Marxism in scripture?

One might argue that we see concern over the superstructure and systems of oppression in the Book of Mormon's references to the Nephite society becoming stratified with class distinctions, with the people having unequal chances for learning. But before we go too far down that path in our thinking, It's important to acknowledge that we can see the idea of superstructure in a lot of non-Marxist thinking. For example, in right-wing American politics there is a narrative that the entertainment industry and academia form a superstructure that oppresses people of faith and keeps people throughout our nation unable to live as their true selves. So it is possible to see a superstructure concept in scripture and other places without concluding that the Marxist worldview is being validated.

Marxism and Scripture

Sometimes Marxist thinkers point to collective, communal society among Christian communities in scripture and claim in response that the gospel is a Marxist belief system. The obvious problem with this is that in communal Christian societies in scripture, participation is not coerced as it is in communism.

Communists know that real communal living requires a new consciousness that is free of the kinds of tendencies that lead toward competitiveness and class identity. The communist solution is to impose this new consciousness on society through mass murder and brainwashing. The Christian solution is very different. Christians can live communally when there is voluntary transformation of perspective that we call *conversion*. And the Christian way is to respect people's decisions to not participate in communal systems of living, rather than to coerce their participation through force.

We do see elements of the tactics of Marxist movements in the Book of Mormon's story of the Gadianton robbers. Mao and other Marxists engaged in guerilla warfare and plunder in their efforts to overthrow society in the service of a communal ideal enforced through violence. It is interesting, then, to read the words of Giddianhi, leader of the Gadianton Robbers, to the Nephite governor Lachoneus. Speaking of his followers, Giddianhi says,

> *And I, knowing of their unconquerable spirit, having proved them in the field of battle, and knowing of their everlasting hatred towards you because of the many wrongs which ye have done unto them, therefore if they should come down against you they would visit you with utter destruction. (3 Ne 3:4)*

The reference to "the many wrongs which ye have done unto them" describes a grievance narrative that has come to motivate this group of robbers.

Giddianhi offers Lachoneus a coercive and confusing choice:

> Therefore I write unto you, desiring that ye would yield up unto this my people, your cities, your lands, and your possessions, rather than that they should visit you with the sword and that destruction should come upon you.
>
> Or in other words, yield yourselves up unto us, and unite with us and become acquainted with our secret works, and become our brethren that ye may be like unto us—not our slaves, but our brethren and partners of all our substance. (3 Ne 3:6-7)

This choice is coercive because in later verses Giddianhi will threaten Lachoneus with the full destruction of the Nephites. The choice is confusing at first, because Giddianhi promises Lachoneus a peaceful existence within his movement. The Nephites can "become our brethren" and share belongings with the Gadianton robbers. How can this utopian picture be squared with the earlier statement that the Gadianton robbers are consumed with an "everlasting hatred?"

The answer to that question solidifies the Gadianton movement as Maoist in nature. Mao demonstrated a Marxist cult of personality, where he could literally shift his followers' narratives and their emotional states with his pronouncements. Giddianhi likewise knew that he had the ability to shift his followers' narrative of the Nephites from a grievance-oriented narrative to one of cooperation. In other words, if he wanted his people to live peacefully with the Nephites, he could personally make that happen. His message to Lachoneus might be rephrased as *see all this hatred my people have toward your people? I can make all that hatred go away*. Whether he would have, is doubtful. But he *could* have.

The invitation to live communally, coupled with the threat of destruction, is precisely what was enacted in the forced collectivizing campaigns of communist China and Russia. In both cases, the rural peasant classes were decimated by authoritarian communist government violence and by famine.

The Millennium and Year Zero

In my initial reading of the book Critical Race Theory, I found myself stunned by a particular passage. The authors wrote,

> The reader will recall that CRT takes liberalism to task for its cautious, incremental quality. When we are tackling a structure as deeply embedded as race, radical measures are required. "Everything must change at once," otherwise the system merely swallows up the small improvement one has made, and everything remains the same.[2]

This was echoed in a social media post I recently saw on X, where climate activist Clover Hogan said,

> The most insidious form of climate denial is no longer, "It's not happening," but the belief that incremental or tech solutions will solve this crisis.[3]

Activists who are steeped in Marxist theory tend to dream of a complete, total, all-at-once transformation of the world. Some of this hearkens back to early Marxist thinkers like Georg Lukacs, who saw in Marxism a notion of *totality*, the idea that everything in society is interconnected. If everything is interconnected, then a failure to change one thing in society will spill over

---

2   Delgado and Stefancic, *Critical Race Theory*. (Kindle locations 664-666)

3   Clover Hogan, "The Most Insidious Form of Climate Denial."

into failures to change other things. It's the social theory equivalent of the old saying that "one rotten apple spoils the whole bunch."

This idea creates in the minds of activists the impression that the whole world needs to be transformed in one instant, with no trace of the former ways of thinking and doing. If that sounds extreme, consider that when the Khmer Rouge took power, they declared "Year Zero," an expression meant to convey that all of Cambodian society was to become completely new, immediately. Here is a summary of what followed:

> Pol Pot declared 1975 to be "Year Zero," when Cambodia was to be isolated and its society remade in accordance with communist ideals. Civil rights and property rights were immediately eliminated, and any public expression of religious belief was forbidden. Taking the view that Cambodian society had been corrupted by exposure to the world beyond Cambodia's borders, the new regime started destroying evidence of Western influence, emptying cities and force-marching the urban population into the countryside to engage in hopelessly inadequate agricultural projects.[4]

The idea of complete renewal of the world did not originate in Marxism. We know that Marx had plenty of exposure to the Bible in his youth, and numerous biblical prophets told of a coming day wherein the world will be renewed. Isaiah told of a time when

> *The wolf also shall dwell with the lamb, and the leopard shall lie down with the kid; and the calf and the young lion and the fatling together; and a little child shall lead them.*

---

4   *Encyclopedia Britannica*, "Cambodian Genocide"

Marxism and Scripture

> *And the cow and the bear shall feed; their young ones shall lie down together: and the lion shall eat straw like the ox.*
>
> *And the sucking child shall play on the hole of the asp, and the weaned child shall put his hand on the cockatrice's den.*
>
> *They shall not hurt nor destroy in all my holy mountain: for the earth shall be full of the knowledge of the Lord, as the waters cover the sea. (Isa 11:6-9)*

Isaiah later offered the prophetic vision that "He will swallow up death in victory; and the Lord God will wipe away tears from off all faces; and the rebuke of his people shall he take away from off all the earth: for the Lord hath spoken it." (Isaiah 25:8)

Likewise, Malachi prophesied:

> *For, behold, the day cometh, that shall burn as an oven; and all the proud, yea, and all that do wickedly, shall be stubble: and the day that cometh shall burn them up, saith the Lord of hosts, that it shall leave them neither root nor branch. (Malachi 4:1)*

Finally, we recall John the Revelator's proclamation that "I saw a new heaven and a new earth: for the first heaven and the first earth were passed away..." (Rev 21:1)

These prophetic statements express clearly that there will come a time when the earth is renewed. Scripture seems to indicate that there will be a fundamental transformation of the way things are. The basic differences between the Christian understanding of this change versus the Marxist understanding of this change have to do with the nature of this future change and the centrality of God's role in bringing it to pass.

Marxists view the great transformation of the world as something that they can bring about, and in this, God is not only irrelevant to the process, but notions of God actually serve as an obstacle to their vision of what is to come. In the Marxist view, enlightened activists bring about the ideal development of human history now and into the future. Christians, on the other hand, view the coming changes as a divine transformation of the world into a peaceful and righteous place, with peace and righteousness established wholly and entirely on God's terms.

Marxism as The Great and Abominable Church

In the March 2015 issue of the Ensign, Elder Dallin H. Oaks wrote:

> Book of Mormon prophecies describe the "great and abominable church of all the earth, whose founder is the devil". This "church" is prophesied to have "dominion over all the earth, among all nations, kindreds, tongues, and people". Called "most abominable above all other churches," this church is also said to act "for the praise of the world" in bringing "the saints of God … down into captivity".
>
> Because no religious denomination—Christian or non-Christian—has ever had "dominion" over all nations of the earth or the potential to bring all the saints of God down into "captivity," this great and abominable church must be something far more pervasive and widespread than a single "church," as we understand that term today. It must be any philosophy or organization that opposes belief in God. And the "captivity" into which this "church" seeks to bring the saints will not be so much physical confinement as the captivity of false ideas.[5]

Elder Oaks' discussion of the Great and Abominable Church in the Book of Mormon was important for a number of reasons. Many Latter-day Saint interpreters

---

5   Oaks, "Stand as Witnesses of God."

of that passage in scripture have looked to specific institutions as being the fulfillment of Nephi's vision, but Elder Oaks offers a broader view that the Great and Abominable Church can take a number of possible forms. It can be a system or a family of systems for which Nephi used the metaphor of a church to convey that this system can organize and spread influence.

With that in mind, how well does Marxism fit the descriptive language of the Great and Abominable Church in Nephi's vision?

To answer that, we need to examine the characteristics of the Great and Abominable Church that Nephi puts forward in his visionary experience related in 1 Nephi 13:

Verse 4: I saw among the nations of the Gentiles the formation of a great church…

Marxism is a system, and it was formed among nations of the gentiles, specifically in Germany and France. Marx was not the originator of all of the ideas in what we call Marxism, but he was the first to systematize those ideas and make them into an action-oriented movement.

Verse 5: Behold the formation of a church which is most abominable above all other churches, which slayeth the saints of God, yea, and tortureth them and bindeth them down, and yoketh them with a yoke of iron, and bringeth them down into captivity.

Here we read that persecution of saints, the followers of Christ, is another key characteristic of the Great and Abominable Church. There is probably no belief system in modern history that has been a greater source of violent persecution of followers of Christ throughout the world, than Marxism and all of its branches.

Verse 6: And it came to pass that I beheld this great and abominable church; and I saw the devil that he was the founder of it.

In chapter 1, we explored the Satan-admiration that was common among Marx and his early associates. In the next chapter we will explore this question of Marxism and satanism in greater depth.

Verses 7-8: And I also saw gold, and silver, and silks, and scarlets, and fine-twined linen, and all manner of precious clothing; and I saw many harlots. And the angel spake unto me, saying: Behold the gold, and the silver, and the silks, and the scarlets, and the fine-twined linen, and the precious clothing, and the harlots, are the desires of this great and abominable church.

Marxist movements typically claim to represent the common worker, the lower classes, the vulnerable in society. But in observable Marxist reality, we see a constant tendency for leaders of Marxist movements to amass power and resources to themselves, and destroy the lower classes of society. Some of the most notable concentrations of Marxist activity are on the campuses of universities with massive layers of administration, and extraordinary financial endowments of donor funding.

In modern-day America, wealthy progressive cities are the locations of the greatest concentrations of people living in extreme economic class inequality, and those cities tend to be led by Marxist-leaning politicians.

Verse 26: And after they go forth by the hand of the twelve apostles of the Lamb, from the Jews unto the Gentiles, thou seest the formation of that great and abominable church, which is most abominable above all other churches; for behold, they have taken away from the gospel of the Lamb many parts which are plain and most

Marxism and Scripture

precious; and also many covenants of the Lord have they taken away.

To take away plain and precious parts of the gospel is often imagined to be a process of changing scripture in ways that obscure God's intended meanings. But another way to think of this passage is to understand how critical readings of scripture remove God from the text entirely. We have mentioned Bruno Bauer and other figures who attacked the bible using their critical tools, and reinterpreted it to remove any notions of miracles up to and including the resurrection of Christ. Critical scholarship of scripture devastates communities of faith by undermining people's confidence in the witnesses of God that we find in scriptural texts. Much of the field of critical scholarship has its origins in Germany during the time of Marx, and Marx had plenty of exposure to critical approaches to the Bible.

Critical scholars often claim to be "unbiased" in their analysis of scripture, compared to religious believers who bring a believing agenda to scripture. Biblical scholar Robert Oden wrote a book called "The Bible Without Theology," where he argued that religious training in biblical studies leaves students with a biased view of the bible, compared to religiously-neutral university environments.

But in a response to Oden, biblical scholar Edgar Conrad wrote that

> Oden has overstated his case here by ignoring the role played by other ideologies such as Marxism and feminism in the university. He has also failed to see that his own positivistic reading is no more objective than historical criticism but is in fact another form of confessional reading. However, Oden's argument that historical-

critical strategies of interpretation have preserved a German tradition of idealism with its inception in the nineteenth century, a tradition that has long since been abandoned by other disciplines, is a helpful one. He provides a useful summary of the characteristics of 'the German tradition of historiography', which 'began to take shape at the end of the eighteenth century, had its peak just before 1850 and then after periods of doubts and competition from other models of understanding was revived in the decades around 1900'. This particular tradition of historiography 'influenced biblical scholars in the nineteenth century and … continues to influence biblical study in the twentieth century'[6]

Edgar Conrad was correct: academic analysis of the bible is every bit as biased and agenda-driven as religious study of the bible. Conrad mentioned Marxism as an influence in academia, but he also referenced Oden's description of German approaches to scholarship that became prominent in the time of Marx and continue into the present day. Marx was swimming in those German intellectual currents, and he made his own significant contribution to them as he developed a worldview that would become pervasive throughout academia.

Denial of miracles and questioning the sources of scripture certainly constitute removal of plain and precious truths from the text, but what about Nephi's mention of the removal of covenants? With Marxism in particular, there emerges a new set of covenants that supersede the ones we find in scripture. Marxism replaces the Christian covenant of repentance with a covenant to reject any spiritual

---

[6] Conrad, "Prophet, Redactor and Audience: Reforming the Notion of Isaiah's Formation", in Melugin and Sweeney, *New Visions of Isaiah*. p.306

authority to define sin. This is called *antinomianism*, or "law-rejection." Marxism replaces the Christian covenant to love one's neighbor with a new covenant to attack and criticize relentlessly in the service of Marxist ideology. Marxism replaces the Christian covenant to love God with a covenant to love political party and specific authoritarian figures with our full devotion. Marxism replaces the Christian covenant to spread the gospel with a new godless covenant of relentless political activism.

These are some examples of the covenant-replacement that comes with Marxism, and numerous other examples could be cited. But together, these and the other characteristics of Marxism that we have explored in this section form a powerful picture of Marxism as an example of the Great and Abominable Church.

At the time of the writing of Robert Payne's 1968 biography of Marx, he noted that half the world was under the rule of governments that based their systems on Marxist thinking. This brings to mind a passage in Doctrine and Covenants that expands upon Jesus' parable of the wheat and tares: "That great church, the mother of abominations, that made all nations drink of the wine of the wrath of her fornication, that persecuteth the saints of God, that shed their blood—she who sitteth upon many waters, and upon the islands of the sea—behold, she is the tares of the earth … ." (D&C 88:94)

The Marxist view of reality did indeed spread over the world—over many waters and the islands of the sea—like wildfire. In recent decades it has become a replacement secular religious system, filling a God- and church- shaped hole in the hearts of people throughout the world who have grown disillusioned with faith. Its primary tool, criticism, contributes to persecution of the saints and leads to the removal of plain and precious meanings of scripture. It has proven to be extremely effective in leading people and societies away from faith in God.

Chapter 9

Marxism and Satanism

To explore Marxism and satanism, we need to return to the process of defining terms. In chapter 1 we defined Marxism in terms of a worldview, and here we will do the same for satanism.

The Satanic Worldview

The worldview held by Satan himself is something that we can piece together primarily through study of scripture, but also through exploring the thinking of modern satanists. If this sounds frightening, I would suggest the reader bear with me. The satanic worldview can be described in simple gospel terms that do not veer into the occult or other areas of spiritual quicksand, and in exploring the satanic worldview we come to see evil in practical terms that demystify it and really empower us to overcome it.

A basic approach to thinking about the conflict between good and evil in the world is to understand that Christ and Satan are both cloning themselves, shaping souls into whichever image that each soul allows. When a soul embraces the influence of Christ, accepts His atonement, and commits to following His gospel, that soul comes to reflect Christ's image of joy, strength, poise, and abundance. By contrast, when a soul embraces the influence of Satan, that soul comes to reflect Satan's image of hostility, despair, insecurity, and emptiness.

In scripture, we see specific instances where Christ and Satan offer their influence to people and groups, and we can observe the consequences of the ways people respond. In the table below, we can see Satan's attempt to exert his influence, and we can map each instance to a corresponding element of his worldview:

Marxism and Satanism

Scripture	Worldview Element
Moses 1:12 And it came to pass that when Moses had said these words, behold, Satan came tempting him, saying: Moses, son of man, worship me.	Deep insecurity, delusion (divinity can be simply asserted/claimed)
Moses 4:1 Behold, here am I, send me, I will be thy son, and I will redeem all mankind, that one soul shall not be lost, and surely I will do it; wherefore give me thine honor.	Egalitarianism, entitlement, delusion (about the nature of reality, the development of souls)
Moses 4:3 ...because that Satan rebelled against me, and sought to destroy the agency of man...	Delusion about the development of souls
Moses 5:38 And Cain said unto the Lord: Satan tempted me because of my brother's flocks. And I was wroth also; for his offering thou didst accept and not mine; my punishment is greater than I can bear.	Jealousy, relativism
Matthew 4:3 And when the tempter came to him, he said, If thou be the Son of God, command that these stones be made bread.	Appetites are to be indulged
Matthew 4:6 And saith unto him, If thou be the Son of God, cast thyself down: for it is written, He shall give his angels charge concerning thee: and in their hands they shall bear thee up, lest at any time thou dash thy foot against a stone.	Craving for affirmation and recognition
Matthew 4:8-9 Again, the devil taketh him up into an exceeding high mountain, and sheweth him all the kingdoms of the world, and the glory of them; And saith unto him, All these things will I give thee, if thou wilt fall down and worship me.	Power is the great objective of life; we should see everything in terms of power relationships and power imbalances
Revelation 12:9-10 And the great dragon was cast out, that old serpent, called the Devil, and Satan, which deceiveth the whole world: he was cast out into the earth, and his angels were cast out with him. And I heard a loud voice saying in heaven, Now is come salvation, and strength, and the kingdom of our God, and the power of his Christ: for the accuser of our brethren is cast down, which accused them before our God day and night.	Accusation is the mechanism for achieving our objectives; the more accusation, the better

In these passages, we see the basic elements of Satan's worldview. If we want to understand evil in the world, we simply need to look through these lenses. Satan believes specific things and feels specific things, and his objective is to thwart God's purposes by causing God's children to adopt that satanic worldview.

Now, let's take each of these worldview elements and explore them in relation to Marxism.

First, we begin with the passage in Moses 1:12 where Satan tells Moses "…son of man, worship me." The first thing to note is that Christ never issued this kind of command; He invites humanity to worship the Father, and He gives glory to the Father. In this, Christ models to the world spiritual wholeness, an understanding of His worth that leaves Him without cravings for recognition. Christ can give glory to the Father because Christ is spiritually well. He knows who He is. He does not need to be constantly reassured and validated.

By contrast, Satan is insecure and emotionally fragile. He has a hard time with the fact that beings like our heavenly parents have glory, but he does not. William Godwin was a radical philosopher who influenced Karl Marx, and Godwin said of Satan,

> Why did he rebel against his maker? It was, as he himself informs us, because he saw no sufficient reason, for that extreme inequality of rank and power which the creator assumed.[1]

As we discussed in chapter 1, this kind of revering of Satan was common in the revolutionary circles where Karl Marx began his university studies and began forming his

---

1   Godwin, *Enquiry Concerning Political Justice*.

own post-Christian worldview. And Godwin was correct; the idea that Satan viewed the disparity between God's glory and Satan's own lack of glory in terms of an unfair inequality shows Satan's sense of entitlement. Satan viewed the kind of glory that God possesses as something that Satan could simply claim or assert without paying the price in personal development.

Rather than accept reality, Satan decided to treat glory and exaltation as something that is simply established between people, or to use terms a present-day neo-Marxist might use, Satan decided that glory was a *social construct*. This is why he sought to have Moses worship him: to treat something as a social construct allows a delusional soul to pretend something is real, and they do that by recruiting other people to participate in their delusion.

Next, we see Satan's worldview in his claim "I will redeem all mankind, that one soul shall not be lost." Satan held a view that it would be possible to impose a single salvational outcome on every soul. We might call this Satan's theory, because that is exactly what he presented: a theory. Satan held the view that *theoretically*, it would be possible to do what he was claiming. His theory was not compatible with God's established reality, the reality that anywhere there is exercise of agency, it is not possible to ensure a single outcome for all.

The set of ideas that we often call Satan's *plan* might have been a plan in the sense of having specific steps, but we don't know. All we have from Satan is a claim that reflected his absolute confidence in his theory. For Satan, there appears to have been no distinction between theory and reality.

Next, we read of God's explanation that Satan "sought to destroy the agency of man." The undermining of agency appears to have been a basic principle in Satan's delusional theory. Satan was under the impression that souls do not need to undergo real development; souls do not need to grow in wisdom through real experience; souls do not need to learn to engage well with reality in the same way God does. Somehow, the prospect of disparate salvational outcomes was so upsetting to Satan that he mentally retreated into unreality and eventually made unreality his permanent intellectual environment.

Next we learn of Satan's worldview through Cain's statement to God following his murder of Abel. Cain says that Satan tempted him because of Abel's flocks. As Satan imparted his influence and his worldview to Cain, Cain became jealous. He felt entitled. Cain further expresses this in his remark to God that "his offering thou didst accept and not mine...", which conveys that under Satan's influence, Cain had become consumed with thoughts of comparison toward his brother Abel. Rather than repent and give an appropriate offering, Cain somehow decided that God's entire system was unfair because his brother was doing better in that system. Cain was becoming a clone of Satan: entitled, unwilling to learn, insisting that reality be something other than what it is, and more.

Next, we consider the first temptation of Christ in the wilderness, where Satan encouraged the fasting Christ to turn the stones around Him into bread. In this example, Satan's message is that cravings are not to be denied. Our lives and activities should be focused on what we desire, and to live otherwise is to not be "authentic."

In the second temptation of Christ, Satan encourages Christ to jump from a high place of the temple in Jerusalem, and then be rescued by angels. This would establish with finality the validity of Christ's mission, leaving no doubt in

His mind or in the mind of anyone else. It would also gain Him a level of recognition and validation that most people crave.

In the third temptation of Christ, Satan offers him the kingdoms of the world if Christ will worship him. In this temptation, Satan is exposing the power-hungry nature of his worldview, the notion that power is the means for bringing about whatever a person seeks to experience or achieve in the world.

In the Old Testament we learn of *hesed*, which is the Hebrew word for "covenant love." Israel is commanded to love God with a different kind of love than the ordinary affections that they feel for their family and friends; *hesed* is a reverent love that involves obligations and also powerful promises.

Hesed seems to be the demand of Satan in the third temptation. And it has been the demand of Marxist tyrants; think of the cults of personality established by Mao, Stalin, Castro, and others. Marxist tyrants assume the role of God in requiring *hesed*, with promises of an ideal society and deliverance from enemies.

Finally, we read in the book of Revelation that Satan was known in premortality as "The accuser of our brothers and sisters…which did accuse them before our God day and night." Here we learn that accusation was Satan's basic orientation toward other people. He had a compulsive craving to tear down other souls, focusing entirely on anything that might be considered a flaw. In the worldview of Satan, sin and flaws and even unmet expectations are the defining characteristic of any person or group or system.

In light of this exploration of the satanic worldview, consider this description of the life of Karl Marx from biographer Robert Payne:

> [Marx] was far from being a paragon of Communist virtues. He went on monumental pub crawls, speculated on the stock exchange, seduced his maidservant, fathered an illegitimate child, dallied with aristocratic young women, and enjoyed his visits to expensive watering places...
>
> He exploited everyone around him-his wife, his children, his mistress and his friends - with a ruthlessness which was all the more terrible because it was deliberate and calculating...
>
> Toward the end of his life he suffered from progressive paranoia, and he would talk about the great revolutionary movements he still controlled, when in fact he had no organized following at all.[2]

Robert Payne's summary conveys entitlement, delusion, self-centeredness, jealousy, craving, and obsession. As we read in scripture, these are all terms that convey the worldview of Satan. They are reflected in the life of Karl Marx.

We wonder if things might have been different for Marx if he had better mentors and associates. It seems like in the most formative period of his life, his young adulthood, he was surrounded by people who ended up steering him in some terrible directions emotionally and intellectually. His early associates seemed to feed his worst instincts, instead of modeling maturity, wellness, and faith. There are profound spiritual lessons in observing how Marx was influenced by a crowd of chaotic and tormented souls, and we contrast his story with that of C. S. Lewis, a great intellect who was influenced in the direction of spiritual development and greatness by a wonderful mentor, J. R.

---

2   Payne, *Marx*. p.12

R. Tolkien. The life of Marx illustrates how the friends we choose can impact us for good or for evil.

Was Marx Possessed?

Numerous biographers and observers of the life of Marx have commented on the manifestations of the demonic in his life, noting in particular his father's concern that Marx had a "demon" (see the discussion in chapter 1). When we describe Marx and the demonic, we tend to use a number of phrases:

- *Marx was possessed*
- *Marx had demons*
- *Marx was under demonic influence*

This reflects the range of ways that we tend to conceptualize the demonic in general. And defenders of Karl Marx are correct to point out that Marx's father was not explicitly stating that Marx was possessed of an evil demon; he was expressing a concern that Karl had a powerful driving influence in his life, and it was unclear whether that influence would lead to good or evil over time.

In our day there is a branch of psychotherapy called Internal Family Systems therapy (IFS), and it can help to shed light on this question of demonic influence on Karl Marx. Developed by therapist Richard Schwartz in the 1980s, IFS treats the human psyche as having multiple "parts," and the parts are to some extent autonomous, like individual people. IFS therapy involves contacting these "parts" and engaging with them as if they are individual people, and helping them to release toxic patterns of thinking and behavior.

In 2023, one of the pioneers of IFS, Bob Falconer, wrote a book called *The Others Within Us*, where he acknowledged the reality that some of the "parts" contacted in IFS therapy are not in fact part of the person's psyche, and they represent what many belief systems have understood to be demonic entities.

Falconer describes a therapeutic encounter with one of these entities, which he calls "unattached burdens:"

> I started working with this woman about this thing in her. It was relentlessly negative. Usually, with an inner critic, you can find out why it's criticizing, such as it wants to keep the person safe or motivate them or improve their lot in life. There's a good intention in there somewhere. We looked for this energy's good intention over and over. I would ask her, "Can you ask this thing why it keeps criticizing you so harshly?" It would just say things like, "I want to cut her down to size." I'd ask, "What's good about cutting her down to size?" "Well, then she wouldn't be so arrogant." "And what's good about her not being arrogant?" "I just want to destroy her." It just kept stating negative things. This is the first important indication that something is not a part of a person's system...This thing didn't seem to have any good intention.[3]

In IFS we see descriptions, in therapeutic terminology, of the range of experiences of the demonic that we mentioned earlier, and it becomes clear that often there is a very blurry line between demonic influence versus possession. In light of lessons learned from IFS, the concern over the nature of the "demon" described by Karl Marx's father makes sense. It is possible to experience the demonic in a variety of ways, and Marx's father seems to

---

3 Falconer, *The Others Within Us*. p.55

have intuited that something may have been influencing his son in powerful ways, even if he could not fully identify the nature of that deep problem within him.

To Love and Make a Lie

In restoration scripture we are told of the telestial world,

> *These are they who are liars, and sorcerers, and adulterers, and whoremongers, and whosoever loves and makes a lie. (D&C 76:103)*

One of the most surprising aspects of neo-Marxism is the many ways that it requires its adherents to lie. Earlier in the book we discussed the understanding of the Frankfurt school and later movements based on critical theory, that truth is not the primary aim of inquiry. Neo-Marxist activism is oriented toward social upheaval, not factual accuracy. For this reason, people who adhere to these movements find themselves constantly saying things that they know are not true.

In our earlier discussion of Critical Race Theory, we mentioned Roland Fryer and how he was persecuted for producing research that did not fit an activist narrative of systemic oppression. Likewise, critical race theorists strenuously avoid questions about how fatherlessness has devastated the socioeconomic mobility of black families in America. By contrast, consider this statement from former president Barack Obama:

> Of all the rocks upon which we build our lives, we are reminded today that family is the most important. And we are called to recognize and honor how critical every father is to that foundation... But if we are honest with ourselves, we'll admit that what too many fathers also

> are is missing—missing from too many lives and too many homes… You and I know how true this is in the African-American community. We know that more than half of all black children live in single parent households, a number that has doubled—doubled—since we were children… And the foundations of our community are weaker because of it.[4]

This was powerful honesty, and it is hard to imagine that years later, the Black Lives Matter movement would explicitly promote the Marxist falsehood that the family is a key element of systemic oppression in society.

In the spirit of loving and making a lie, queer theory and gender theory likewise require their adherents to profess a belief that people with fake, surgically-constructed body parts, or gender-stereotypical costumes, are now a biological sex different from their birth sex. According to queer and gender theory, this is an identity that the rest of the world is obligated to accept.

To love and make a lie is to insist that reality is something other than what it really is. Marxist movements are made up of many people who profess an anti-authoritarian worldview, and yet these same Marxist movements have a perfect historical record of putting into power some of history's most vicious tyrants. This is not an accidental outcome; it is part of the basic design of Marxism.

To understand this by way of analogy, imagine that a community approves the construction of a car factory in their area. When the factory is built, it has a large sign advertising the new cars it will be producing. And yet, when people are hired to work in the factory, they find

---

4   Politico, "Text of Obama's Fatherhood Speech."

Marxism and Satanism

themselves working on an assembly line that produces toaster ovens. In this situation, obviously there is a mismatch between the advertised claims of the factory, versus the basic design for its production line. It does not matter what the factory advertises; what it actually produces — whether cars or toasters — is a question of its internal design.

People who work in that factory who were hoping to produce cars might reassure themselves that someday the factory will produce cars. But that would not be possible without a fundamentally different factory design. At some point, those people would need to face reality squarely and ask those basic hard questions around design.

Likewise, Marxists who hold a fantasy of an egalitarian society that cares for the poor and marginalized are faced with basic questions around the design of their belief system, and how it always produces the opposite of what it advertises, the society they hope for.

I will note that in preparation for this book, I have consumed a significant amount of Marxist materials, both written and audiovisual media. One of the most surprising things in that process has been watching Marxists defend the actions of Lenin, Mao, and others. Recall that we discussed earlier the story of Erich Fromm in the Frankfurt School, and his conflicts with others there over his research showing that authoritarianism is not an exclusively right-wing phenomenon. With all we have been able to observe of the history of Marxism, nothing could be more clearly obvious than that Marxist movements always produce authoritarianism.

It has been shocking, then, to see how Marxists offer apologetics for authoritarian figures and excuse them. Sometimes they even celebrate the actions of these authoritarians, when they condemn those same actions among people of opposing political movements.

Recall that at the beginning of this book, we referred to Jonathan Haidt's conservative and liberal groupings of moral intuitions:

Conservative intuitions:
- Loyalty/betrayal
- Authority/subversion
- Sanctity/degradation

Liberal/progressive intuitions:
- Care/harm
- Fairness/cheating

When a Marxist claims to reject authority-based intuitions, but then embraces those intuitions when they are manifest among other Marxists, this is called *partisan morality*. When a person's sense of morality becomes partisan, the question of whether something is right or wrong becomes determined by which team is doing it. In another example, if a Marxist claims to hold their views out of a moral sense of care for the marginalized and oppressed, and he then excuses or ignores Marxist oppression carried out by Lenin and Mao and others, then his morality is partisan.

For a final example of this, one often stated by critical race theorists in particular, consider the phrase "only white people can be racist." This phrase, together with all of the bizarre mental gymnastics and redefinitions of terms that are used to support it, serve to deny a significant dimension of moral agency to anyone except white people. The truth is that people of all races can be racist. So people who engage in the partisan framing of morality that enables the statement "only white people can be racist," are required to employ academic tools to deny realities that are observably true. Returning to scriptural language, this is a partisan example of what it means to love and make a lie.

And here we need to be clear: *partisan morality is no morality*. God's intentions for His children are to develop an internal sense of morality that aligns with the realities of the universe, and God's commandments exist to aid in our development of those moral intuitions. When our moral judgments are partisan, this eliminates in our souls the sense that anything is actually right or wrong, good or bad. What is morally right and good is determined by our political team, not by God's law.

The nature of the moral agency that God wishes for us to develop is the exact opposite. For example, in living the restored gospel, we sustain our leaders. This means supporting them and upholding them. But in situations where our leaders have lapses in moral judgment, we don't need to pretend that a lapse was moral just because it occurred on our team. We can grieve moral failures among people we sustain and revere, and give them grace to learn and grow. This is an honest exercise of our moral agency that requires zero compromise of our moral integrity.

By contrast, partisan morality – the kind that excuses the horrible oppression of people like Lenin and Mao – makes it impossible to exercise moral agency because *in the partisan heart, nothing is inherently moral or immoral*. Morality is only a question of what advances our team's quest for power. This is why partisan morality is more properly called partisan *amorality*. In restoration scripture we are taught that Satan seeks to destroy our moral agency (Moses 4:3), and the development of partisan amorality is a way that he accomplishes this objective.

This is another way in which maintaining the historical and moral narratives of classical Marxism, and now the narratives of neo-Marxism and all of its fruits, requires a tremendous amount of lying. Sometimes that lying is in the service of a toxic empathy, or a delusional notion of social justice, or a desire to be viewed as ideologically aligned with a person or group, or any number of other factors. But whatever the motives, there is no question that Marxist ideology requires ever-increasing levels of lying, and that is a satanic process that ends up corroding the souls of people who embrace it over time.

On Criticism and Accusation

At this point, we are getting closer to a more thorough answer to the question of whether Marxism is satanic. But we are not done painting the picture; recall the scriptural description of Satan as the accuser, and then we return once again to Marx's declaration:

> The criticism of religion disillusions man, so that he will think, act, and fashion his reality like a man who has discarded his illusions and regained his senses, so that he will move around himself as his own true Sun. Religion is only the illusory Sun which revolves around man as long as he does not revolve around himself.[5]

In the mind of Marx, religion was to be criticized, which involves accusation toward religious figures and negation of the scriptural witness of God. And contrary to the well-intentioned thinking of some religious reformers throughout history, criticism of religion from the Marxist

---

5   Marx, "A Contribution to the Critique of Hegel's Philosophy of Right 1844."

Marxism and Satanism

worldview comes to fruition not with the reform of religion, but with the *elimination* of religion. Marx expressed this with clarity:

> …it is all the more clear what we have to accomplish at present: I am referring to ruthless criticism of all that exists…
>
> Criticism is no passion of the head, it is the head of passion. It is not a lancet, it is a weapon. Its object is its enemy, which it wants not to refute but to exterminate… Criticism does not need to make things clear to itself as regards this object, for it has already settled accounts with it. It no longer assumes the quality of an end-in-itself, but only of a means. Its essential pathos is indignation, its essential work is denunciation.[6]

It is important to understand that a culture of accusation is not at all unique to Marxism and other left-wing ideologies. In our earlier discussion of Marxism and fascism, we established that the extreme right and left tend to mirror each other. This is especially plain to see in their strategies and tactics, one of which is to develop a culture of accusation that keeps people in a constant state of fear.

In 1997, The Journal of Modern History held a symposium on denunciation as a practice employed in European societies as a means of imposing and maintaining social control. Papers from the symposium were compiled into the book *Accusatory Practices: Denunciation in Modern European History*. The studies in that book illustrate how accusation in its various forms has enabled people in otherwise peaceful societies to abandon the mental and spiritual safeguards that had once allowed

---

6   Ibid.

them to peacefully coexist with their neighbors. The authors introduce the concept by explaining that

> Police, revolutionary, and theocratic states and communities—as well as twentieth-century totalitarian states—have been particularly likely to encourage their citizens or members to write denunciations against each other for purposes of maintaining social control, ideological purity, virtue, and so on. The zealous hunt for heretics, witches, counterrevolutionaries, and other deviants periodically reaches a pitch of collective hysteria when waves of denunciation for fantastic offenses flood in to the authorities...[7]

The studies in *Accusatory Practices* examine European history from the Spanish Inquisition to the French Revolution to pre-Soviet Russia, and on to more recent 20th century Marxist and Fascist regimes. The authors use extensive historical examples to demonstrate that tyrants do not simply impose terror from their official positions atop society; they create chains of participation in terror that stretch to communities and even households. The authors chronicle the importance of accusation in control-oriented ideological movements of the right and left, both religious and irreligious.

As Henry Charles Lea said of denunciation in the Spanish Inquisition, "No more ingenious device has been invented to subjugate a whole populace, to paralyze its intellect, and to reduce it to blind obedience . . . it filled the land with spies and it rendered every man an object of suspicion, not only to his neighbor but to the members of

---

[7] Fitzpatrick and Gellately, *Accusatory Practices*. p. 15

his own family and to the stranger whom he might chance to meet."[8]

Beyond Europe, we know that in the Maoist Cultural Revolution, China was consumed with a wave of accusation and violence against intellectuals and persons perceived to be in positions of privilege. As we noted earlier in our discussion of Maoist China, numerous historical accounts relate that, in what Latter-day Saints might regard as a perfect inverse of our work of redemption of the dead, participants in Mao's Cultural Revolution went so far as to desecrate tombs and engage in denunciations of exhumed corpses of the deceased.

Here we should contrast these coercive satanic strategies of accusation with a legitimate gospel perspective on criticism. In a May 1986 address, Elder Dallin H. Oaks taught that

> The counsel to avoid destructive personal criticism does not mean that Latter-day Saints need to be docile or indifferent to defective policies, deficient practices, or wrongful conduct in government or in private organizations in which we have an interest. Our religious philosophy poses no obstacle to constructive criticism of such conditions. The gospel message is a continuing constructive criticism of all that is wretched or sordid in society. But Christians who are commanded to be charitable and to "[speak] the truth in love" (Eph. 4:15) should avoid personal attacks and shrill denunciations. Our public communications—even those protesting against deficiencies—should be reasoned in content and positive in spirit.[9]

---

8   Ibid., p. 19

9   Dallin H. Oaks, "Criticism"

Elder Oaks' admonition is clear- if criticism is necessary, it should be done with an intent to edify. By contrast, recall that in chapter 1 we noted Marx's affinity for the demonic figure Mephistopheles in Goethe's play *Faust*, in particular Mephistopheles' statement that "All that exists deserves to perish". When we couple that with Marx's poetry and its references to world-destruction, his understanding of the nature of criticism emerges. Consider this pair of phrases from Marx,

"…ruthless criticism of all that exists…"

And,

"…not to refute but to exterminate…"

These are a pair of concepts that convey a total hatred of reality itself, an inability to abide the very existence of the world as we know it. Unlike misotheism, which is a hatred for God, there is no single term for *everything-hatred*, or for *reality-hatred*. And though it is doubtful that all people who hold a Marxist worldview share Marx's personal hatred of reality, that hatred was a very noticeable psychological current that occasionally bubbled up to the surface in Marx's writings.

Marxism, Modern Satanism, and Self as God

Common modern notions of Satanism envision worship of Satan, occult rituals, pentagrams, and even statues of a strange goat-headed being called Baphomet. But a more accurate description of what Satanism really involves is found in the words of Blanche Barton, the "Magistra Templi Rex" of the Church of Satan:

> The idea of worshiping Satan is ridiculous. We worship ourselves first and foremost, and we use the Satanic as a metaphor for calling forth the powers within ourselves

that we find enriching or enlivening. Satan has always been a metaphor of defiance, fortitude against all odds, and self-determination in whatever guises he is represented.[10]

The man regarded as the godfather of modern satanism was Aleister Crowley, an occultist who claimed to receive from a supernatural being a set of teachings called The Book of The Law. This formed the foundation for Thelema, Crowley's belief system named after the Greek word for "self." These teachings have been foundational to modern Satanism.

The most famous teaching in The Book of The Law was a very simple statement: "Do what thou wilt shall be the whole of the law." This phrase was inscribed on some early vinyl records of the hard rock band Led Zeppelin. But in response to numerous questions, Led Zeppelin guitarist Jimmy Page would later say what he found most appealing about Crowley's ideas, and it was the notion of "self-liberation." In a 1977 interview, Page stated that "what I can relate to is Crowley's system of self-liberation, in which repression is the greatest work of sin."

In an article on Crowley and modern Satanism, Asbjorn Dyrendal explains that "[Crowley's] discourse makes use of and contributes to a literary tradition of positive discourse on Satan, and it is central to the disembedding of Satan from Christian demonology and re-embedding him into an esoteric discourse as something positive."[11]

---

10 Monroe-Kane, "The Not-So-Subtle Subversiveness Of Satan Worship."

11 Bogdan and Starr, *Aleister Crowley and Western Esotericism*. p.370

And what is that something positive? It is self-worship, the insistence that one's desires ought to never be "repressed" by culture or religion, seeing that as the "greatest...sin." Or, as satanist rock star Marilyn Manson famously described the core of Satanism, it is about "being your own god."[12]

Returning to our question of whether Marxism is satanic, we can point to a clear answer. To the extent that Marxism leads to antinomianism – a rejection of God's law – and to the extent that Marxism leads us to, in Marx's metaphor, *revolve around ourselves like the sun*, the answer is clearly yes.

---

12 YouTube, "Marilyn Manson Explains Satanism, Aleister Crowley, Anton LaVey."

Conclusion

Marxism and the Plans of Old

We began this book by exploring how Marxism arose in response to specific things: real problems in capitalist societies, and real personal factors in the life of Karl Marx and among the people who influenced him. As we conclude, we need to revisit these issues and see a larger set of tendencies at work in capitalism and in the Marxist response to it.

The most powerful critic of Marxism in history was Aleksandr Solzhenitsyn, who was imprisoned for 16 years in one of Stalin's labor camp "gulags." Upon his release, Solzhenitsyn wrote extensively about the Marxist horror that had consumed Russia for decades. In a legendary 1983 address accepting the Templeton Prize, Solzhenitsyn publicly recognized the misotheistic nature of Marxist movements:

> ...the world had never before known a godlessness as organized, militarized, and tenaciously malevolent as that preached by Marxism. Within the philosophical system of Marx and Lenin and at the heart of their psychology, hatred of God is the principal driving

> force, more fundamental than all their political and economic pretensions. Militant atheism is not merely incidental or marginal to communist policy; it is not a side effect, but the central pivot. To achieve its diabolic ends, communism needs to control a population devoid of religious and national feeling, and this entails a destruction of faith and nationhood. Communists proclaim both of these objectives openly, and just as openly put them into practice.[1]

This is a very accurate assessment, and people who are living happily in capitalist societies will find in Solzhenitsyn's thinking plenty of validation for our sense of the evils of Marxism. Where some commentators view the Marxist elements of their university educations as a positive rite of passage, a commentator like Solzhenitsyn refutes those notions with a deep moral clarity that comes from firsthand experience.

Solzshenitsyn Challenges the West

But this is only part of Solzhenitsyn's remarks, and other of his remarks might cause some profound discomfort for those of us who are inclined to offer uncritical praise of capitalism. During the time of Solzhenitsyn's speech, it was common to refer to the world as divided into the U.S.-led West, and the Russia-led East. In that framing, Solzhenitsyn turned his focus to the free and prosperous capitalist societies of the West, and he was very clear and forthright in his assessment:

> Such incitements to hatred are coming to characterize today's free world. Indeed, the broader the personal

---

1 Templeton Prize, "Acceptance Address by Mr. Aleksandr Solzhenitsyn."

freedoms are, the higher the level of prosperity or even abundance, the more vehement, paradoxically, is this blind hatred. The contemporary developed West thus demonstrates by its own example that human salvation can be found neither in the profusion of material goods nor in merely making money.

This unquenchable hatred then spreads to all that is alive, to life itself, to the world with its colours, sounds and shapes, to the human body…

And here again, the same result is produced both in East and West, through a world-wide process, by the same cause: that men have forgotten God.[2]

What Solzhenitsyn described was a tendency for the two polarities of Marxism and capitalism to become destructive, each in their own ways. This obviously poses a hard question for those of us in the West: in what sense is capitalism destructive?

A simple answer is that capitalism leads to something we call "creative destruction." In their pursuit of capital, people in capitalist societies create industries that eliminate other industries in a competitive marketplace. Capitalism is a system of constant destruction and upheaval, that is ideally balanced by creation: creation of new wealth, new ideas, new industries. Generally, this works. And if our measure of the value of an economic system is its ability to create material prosperity, then capitalism works better than any other system.

This is why non-capitalist countries face constant challenges of immigration outflows, whereas capitalist countries face constant challenges of managing immigration *inflows*. Marxism thinks that most people

---

2   Ibid.

should want to live without class distinctions and private property, but in reality most people really just want to live where they have the best chance to prosper.

U2 singer Bono has devoted his life to social activism, and much of his efforts have tended to be left-leaning. This is why many people were surprised to read his thoughts in an October 2022 interview with the New York Times:

> I ended up as an activist in a very different place from where I started. I thought that if we just redistributed resources, then we could solve every problem. I now know that's not true. There's a funny moment when you realize that as an activist: The off-ramp out of extreme poverty is, ugh, commerce, it's entrepreneurial capitalism.[3]

To reiterate: if our measure of the value of an economic system is its ability to create material prosperity, then capitalism works better than any other system. But Solzhenitsyn mentioned that Western capitalist systems had created new kinds of hatreds, "to all that is alive, to life itself, to the world with its colours, sounds and shapes, to the human body…"

How is it possible that a system that creates prosperity also creates "hatreds" and misery?

At several points in this book, we discussed the Marxist template for understanding society, that identifies certain things as private property. Access to private property then becomes viewed as exclusive, maintained for a certain class of people through systems of oppression. The Marxist solution to this problem is to eliminate the private nature of that property, either by overthrowing the systems of oppression that maintain limited access to the property, or

---

3 Marchese, "Bono Is Still Trying to Figure Out U2 and Himself."

by criticizing the actual property itself in ways that ensure it can no longer be held by any single group.

Applying this template, where capital is the exclusively-held property, the Marxist program is to confiscate and redistribute. Where according to critical race theorists "whiteness" is the exclusively-held property, the neo-Marxist program is to enact policies that confiscate and redistribute privilege. Where according to queer and gender theorists "normal" is the exclusively-held property, the neo-Marxist program is to apply critical theory and obliterate norms so that no one can hold the property of "normal." The tools of critical theory are designed to bring about the redistribution or the destruction of anything that is considered to be property.

One of the problems with capitalism is that it tends to be chameleonic, taking upon itself even the form of Marxism in order to open up new markets for goods and services. In earlier chapters, we mentioned how capitalism allows people to access private properties like race and gender for a price. Tanning beds, surgeries, drugs, and body-modification clothing are all examples of products that allow people access to neo-Marxist "properties" of race and gender, for a price.

In her book *Feminism Against Progress*, writer Mary Harrington offers feminism and patriarchy as an example of this formula. Where patriarchy is viewed by many feminists as a system of oppression that maintains exclusive privileges for men over women, Harrington discusses a history of feminist thought that considered communism to be the answer, allowing for state control of children and other factors that create social imbalances between men and women. Harrington notes, however, that communism did not provide the solution: capitalism did, in the form of birth control technology.

> ... the philosopher Simone de Beauvoir, envisaged in her groundbreaking 1949 feminist classic The Second Sex the same parity of working personhood for both sexes, under communism. To Kollontai's vision of equal access to work, de Beauvoir added that in liberating women from the material consequences of sex, i.e. child-rearing, communism would also grant us equal sexual freedom. In her vision, 'erotic freedom would be accepted by custom [...] marriage would be based on a free engagement that the spouses could break when they wanted to; motherhood would be freely chosen – that is, birth control and abortion would be allowed – and in return all mothers and their children would be given the same rights'. In the end, though, it wasn't communism but technology that delivered.[4]

Harrington offers clear examples of how capitalist forces tend to insinuate themselves into Marxist narratives and present alternatives to the communist visions of revolution and redistribution. Marx understood alienation as a separation from our authentic self that comes with laboring on behalf of others, and this could only be solved by eliminating that relationship of labor to ownership. Capitalism is all too happy to recognize alienation as a problem that takes the form Marx described, but also other forms that are more cultural. And the answer offered by capitalism is to empower people to purchase their way out of any form of alienation using money.

The great Christian writer G.K. Chesterton offered this critique of capitalism:

---

[4] Harrington, *Feminism against Progress*. p.61

Marxism and the Plans of Old

> It cannot be too often repeated that what destroyed the Family in the modern world was Capitalism. No doubt it might have been Communism, if Communism had ever had a chance, outside that semi-Mongolian wilderness where it actually flourishes. But, so far as we are concerned, what has broken up households and encouraged divorces, and treated the old domestic virtues with more and more open contempt, is the epoch and Power of Capitalism. It is Capitalism that has forced a moral feud and a commercial competition between the sexes; that has destroyed the influence of the parent in favour of the influence of the employer; that has driven men from their homes to look for jobs; that has forced them to live near their factories or their firms instead of near their families; and, above all, that has encouraged, for commercial reasons, a parade of publicity and garish novelty, which is in its nature the death of all that was called dignity and modesty by our mothers and fathers.[5]

Chesterton's concerns about capitalism express the reality that there are consequences to the pursuit of wealth and the "creative destruction" that takes place in market economies. Brigham Young placed wealth and its consequences as his greatest concern for the Latter-day Saints:

> The worst fear I have about this people is that they will get rich in this country, forget God and His people, wax fat, and kick themselves out of the Church and go to hell. This people will stand mobbing, robbing, poverty, and all manner of persecutions, and be true. But my greater fear . . . is that they cannot stand wealth.[6]

---

5 Chesterton, *The Well and the Shallows*. p.212

6 Deseret News, "Seek First the Kingdom of God"

It is important to be clear that none of these commentators reject capitalism, but they are very clear and earnest in their views that there are real dangers in wealth and its effects upon people and society. When Brigham Young associated wealth with loss of faith in God, he was prophetically articulating what Aleksandr Solzhenitsyn would say so many years later, that "the same result is produced both in East and West, through a world-wide process, by the same cause: that men have forgotten God."

All of this is to say that many of us are willing to point out the destructive power of Marxism, but hopefully as Latter-day Saints we can have the integrity to share the clarity of Brigham Young and many other great spiritual leaders in understanding that contrary to the messaging we often receive in capitalist societies, the very most important things in life and in eternity cannot be purchased with money, and are often obtained in spite of it.

The Division Into Two

In the Book of Mormon we witness patterns, and two of those patterns are especially relevant to the Marxist history we have covered in this book.

The first pattern involves the recovery of ancient plans around the acquisition of wealth and power:

> *And it came to pass that she did talk with her father, and said unto him: Whereby hath my father so much sorrow? Hath he not read the record which our fathers brought across the great deep? Behold, is there not an account concerning them of old, that they by their secret plans did obtain kingdoms and great glory? (Ether 8:9)*
>
> *Therefore ye shall keep these secret plans of their oaths and their covenants from this people, and only their wickedness and their*

Marxism and the Plans of Old

> *murders and their abominations shall ye make known unto them...*
>
> *And now, my son, remember the words which I have spoken unto you; trust not those secret plans unto this people, but teach them an everlasting hatred against sin and iniquity. (Alma 37:29, 32)*

The second pattern involves the division of people into exactly two warring camps:

> *And it came to pass that the people began to flock together in armies, throughout all the face of the land.*
>
> *And they were divided; and a part of them fled to the army of Shiz, and a part of them fled to the army of Coriantumr. (Ether 14:19-20)*
>
> *And I, Mormon, wrote an epistle unto the king of the Lamanites, and desired of him that he would grant unto us that we might gather together our people unto the land of Cumorah, by a hill which was called Cumorah, and there we could give them battle.*
>
> *And it came to pass that the king of the Lamanites did grant unto me the thing which I desired. (Mormon 6:2-3)*

The secret plans are oriented toward the acquisition of power, and they lead people to enter into conflicts where people perceive only two options available to them: align with exactly one team in the conflict, or the other. In the case of the Jaredites, we are told that the war created by this division laid waste to entire cities, and in this we see the real satanic objective of the plans of old: they do not exist to create a team that will vanquish another team; they exist to lay waste to all of the world as we know it.

In the past century, think of instances where people have been led to divide themselves into exactly two warring camps:

- Proletariat versus Bourgeois (Marxism)
- Communists versus Fascists (WWII-era Europe)

- Axis vs. Allies (WWII)
- Revolutionaries versus Nationalists (Maoist China)
- Revolutionaries versus Capitalists (Maoist China)
- Supporters of terror versus supporters of the war on terror (America following 9/11)
- Righteous supporters of the good presidential candidate versus unrighteous supporters of the evil political candidate (American politics in the present day)

I mention this last example so that American readers in particular can beware of political messaging that is designed to create the illusion that hope for the future is only to be found in one of two possible godless visions for society. That perspective is an ancient trap, and the Book of Mormon helps us to avoid stepping into it.

The Real Division

And as Latter-day Saints, let's be clear- we do have prophetic statements that describe movement toward two possibilities. But they are not the two possibilities that tend to be presented to us in political messaging. In Doctrine and Covenants we read,

> *And it shall come to pass among the wicked, that every man that will not take his sword against his neighbor must needs flee unto Zion for safety.*
>
> *And there shall be gathered unto it out of every nation under heaven; and it shall be the only people that shall not be at war one with another.*
>
> *And it shall be said among the wicked: Let us not go up to battle against Zion, for the inhabitants of Zion are terrible; wherefore we cannot stand.*

Marxism and the Plans of Old

And it shall come to pass that the righteous shall be gathered out from among all nations, and shall come to Zion, singing with songs of everlasting joy. (D&C 45:68-71)

Here in this passage we read of a time when the wicked will be consumed with violence, and the alternative to this violence will be Zion. We do see divisions into two in these verses: ungathered versus gathered, and the wicked versus Zion. These are different divisions than the ones being created by political leaders throughout the world.

We began this book quoting President Ezra Taft Benson, specifically his remarkable 1988 General Conference talk *I Testify*. Here we will revisit and further explore that talk and President Benson's warning to the membership of the church:

> I testify that wickedness is rapidly expanding in every segment of our society. It is more highly organized, more cleverly disguised, and more powerfully promoted than ever before. Secret combinations lusting for power, gain, and glory are flourishing. A secret combination that seeks to overthrow the freedom of all lands, nations, and countries is increasing its evil influence and control over America and the entire world.[7]

Given President Benson's many condemnations of communism as an apostle, we might interpret these remarks as a warning against communism specifically. But I suggest that we think bigger. I suggest that President Benson was warning us about the plans of old, that divide societies into exactly two warring groups and lay waste to the world. Marxism has been the most prominent and lasting ideology to achieve this horror in the last century, but we would do well to understand that other ideologies

---

[7] Ezra Taft Benson, "I Testify"

like fascism are every bit as capable of bringing this satanic vision to fruition. I believe President Benson was warning the church of this larger threat of dividing the world into two warring groups.

And President Benson also offered the church great reasons for hope and confidence. He said in the same talk,

> I testify that the church and kingdom of God is increasing in strength. Its numbers are growing, as is the faithfulness of its faithful members. It has never been better organized or equipped to perform its divine mission.

President Benson's description of the church provides a powerful and beautiful contrast with his warning of the great secret combination. And he continued to prophesy of the church's role. Though the world might envision a great conflict that is resolved through violence between two groups, President Benson offered a different and more inspired narrative:

> I testify that as the forces of evil increase under Lucifer's leadership and as the forces of good increase under the leadership of Jesus Christ, there will be growing battles between the two until the final confrontation. As the issues become clearer and more obvious, all mankind will eventually be required to align themselves either for the kingdom of God or for the kingdom of the devil. As these conflicts rage, either secretly or openly, the righteous will be tested. God's wrath will soon shake the nations of the earth and will be poured out on the wicked without measure. But God will provide strength for the righteous and the means of escape; and eventually and finally truth will triumph.[8]

---

8   Ibid.

Marxism and the Plans of Old

When President Benson spoke of the issues becoming clearer, and all of mankind aligning ourselves with the kingdom of God or the kingdom of the devil, it is important to understand that we as members of the Savior's church have an essential role to play in bringing that clarity to the world. Earlier we read some strong critiques of capitalism, but among those of us who live in capitalist systems, it would be a great mistake to conclude that because there are problems in capitalism, it is no better than Marxism or other social systems.

It is true that in capitalist systems, markets are providing people with access to sexual sin, political corruption, gender surgeries, and countless other awful things that are bought with money. But it is also true that in our capitalist systems, we are best equipped to heed President Benson's directive to the church: "It is time for us, as members of the Church, to walk in all the ways of the Lord, to use our influence to make popular that which is sound and to make unpopular that which is unsound." To make things popular, as President Benson indicated, is to use our influence to show people that there are better alternatives for their lives than to spend money on things that will destroy their souls.

Living as faithful members of Christ's church in capitalist societies, we can take to heart President Benson's admonitions, and that means opposing evil ideologies, but also showing the world what it means to live spiritually well in capitalism. It means showing by the way we use our time and resources that, in the words of Aleksandr Solzhenitsyn,

> ...the meaning of earthly existence lies not, as we have grown used to thinking, in prospering, but in the

development of the soul.[9]

We conclude by returning to a question at the beginning of this book. In light of all of the terrible experiences of Marxism in modern world history, how are church members to feel about doing temple work for ancestors who participated in Marxist movements? The answer to that question is that those ancestors are redeemed by our Christ. His grace is sufficient, and I do not offer that phrase lightly. It is the most weighty and powerful reality that we can consider as we ponder these questions. Every reader of this book should understand that your ancestors are receiving missionaries on the other side of the veil, and I like to imagine that President Benson is among that missionary force. Your ancestors are being taught the gospel. And like all souls who have ever lived, those ancestors are having to unlearn some things that they learned in mortality, including what an ideal society looks like and how it is achieved.

When the spirits of your ancestors ask their missionaries to see what an ideal society looks like, they are not being shown the sacred spaces of capitalism, like smartphone factories or Wall Street. When those spirits ask what an ideal society looks like, they are being given glimpses of the insides of our temples, where the blessings of capitalism have been consecrated for the work of gathering and redeeming all of our brothers and sisters. Your ancestors are being shown you, performing service to them and to God in those sacred spaces. This is how some of the deepest wounds of world history are being healed, one by one, with each passing day.

---

[9] Solzhenitsyn, *The Gulag Archipelago Volume 2*. p.744

Works Cited

Anderson, Jervis. "Cornel West, the Public Intellectual | The New Yorker." Accessed June 11, 2024. https://www.newyorker.com/magazine/1994/01/17/cornel-west-the-public-intellectual.

Andreae, Graham. "Trouble Was Already Brewing at Kendi's Anti-Racism Center in 2021." American Council of Trustees and Alumni (blog), September 28, 2023. https://www.goacta.org/2023/09/trouble-was-already-brewing-at-kendis-anti-racism-center-in-2021/.

Arab News. "Top Khmer Rouge Leader Tells Court He Fought for 'Social Justice.'" February 18, 2016. https://www.arabnews.com/world/news/882401.

Awkward Apologies from White People - Key & Peele, 2019. https://www.youtube.com/watch?v=zrhWLfmfZ0Y.

Backer, Ryan. "Age Queer." ChangingAging (blog), April 7, 2020. https://changingaging.org/ageism/age-queer/.

Bailey, Alison. "Tracking Privilege-Preserving Epistemic Pushback in Feminist and Critical Race Philosophy Classes." Hypatia 32 (September 8, 2017). https://doi.org/10.1111/hypa.12354.

Bakunin, Mikhail. "God and the State - Chapter I." Accessed June 11, 2024. https://www.marxists.org/reference/archive/bakunin/works/godstate/ch01.htm.

Bauer, B. Das Entdeckte Christentum: Eine Erinnerung an Das Neunzehnte Jahrhundert, 1843. https://books.google.com/books?id=NNonSQAACAAJ.

Benson, Ezra Taft. "I Testify." Accessed June 11, 2024. https://www.churchofjesuschrist.org/study/eng/general-conference/1988/10/i-testify.

Biggar, N. Colonialism: A Moral Reckoning. HarperCollins Publishers, 2023. https://books.google.com/books?id=XopbEAAAQBAJ.

Billboard Chris. "Masked Antifa Man." Tweet. Twitter, November 4, 2023. https://x.com/BillboardChris/status/1720919554593845510.

Bogdan, H., and M.P. Starr. Aleister Crowley and Western Esotericism. Oxford University Press, 2012. https://books.google.com/books?id=zOJoAgAAQBAJ.

Butler, Judith. "Merely Cultural." New Left Review, no. I/227 (February 1, 1998): 33–44.

Cadet, Peggy. "Intersex Pretenders." Archives of Sexual Behavior 53, no. 5 (May 1, 2024): 1667–79. https://doi.org/10.1007/s10508-024-02854-0.

Works Cited

"Cambodian Genocide | Description, Killing Fields, & Facts | Britannica." Accessed June 11, 2024. https://www.britannica.com/event/Cambodian-Genocide.

Chang, J. Wild Swans: Three Daughters of China. Simon & Schuster, 2008. https://books.google.com/books?id=0sBu1Fj4Ed0C.

Chesterton, G.K. The Well and the Shallows. Read Books Limited, 2015. https://books.google.com/books?id=nb19CgAAQBAJ.

Clover Hogan. "The Most Insidious Form of Climate Denial." Tweet. Twitter, April 25, 2024. https://x.com/cloverhogan/status/1783429995852964162.

Conrad, Alison. "Identifying and Countering White Supremacy Culture in Food Systems." World Food Policy Center (blog). Accessed June 11, 2024. https://wfpc.sanford.duke.edu/reports/identifying-and-countering-white-supremacy-culture-in-food-systems/.

Dansky, K. The Reckoning: How the Democrats and the Left Betrayed Women and Girls. Bombardier Books, 2023. https://books.google.com/books?id=f7bnEAAAQBAJ.

Delgado, R., and J. Stefancic. Critical Race Theory: An Introduction, Second Edition. Critical America. NYU Press, 2012. https://books.google.com/books?id=p-DInbMLvhgC.

Delgado, Richard. "Rodrigo's Eleventh Chronicle: Empathy and False Empathy Chronicle." Cal L. Rev. 84 (January 1, 1996): 61.

Demunsereeuw, Filip. Deconstructing Karl Marx & Communism: Character Study & Metaphysical Analysis of Communism. Kindle. Minnow Productions, 2023.

DiAngelo, R., and M.E. Dyson. White Fragility: Why It's So Hard for White People to Talk About Racism. Beacon Press, 2018. https://books.google.com/books?id=ZfQ3DwAAQBAJ.

Dixon, Gregg Marcel. "When It Comes to Immigration Reform, Don't Forget Black Voters | Opinion - Newsweek." Accessed June 11, 2024. https://www.newsweek.com/when-it-comes-immigration-reform-dont-forget-black-voters-opinion-1859992.

Editor, Don L. Searle Assistant. "President Ezra Taft Benson Ordained Thirteenth President of the Church." Accessed June 11, 2024. https://www.churchofjesuschrist.org/study/eng/ensign/1985/12/president-ezra-taft-benson-ordained-thirteenth-president-of-the-church.

Ellsworth, Dan. "And Not One Soul Shall Feel Excluded." Public Square Magazine, August 6, 2020. https://publicsquaremag.org/dialogue/and-not-one-soul-shall-feel-excluded/.

Ellsworth, Dan. "Empathy in Modern Culture: A Balanced Perspective." Public Square Magazine, November 20, 2023. https://publicsquaremag.org/faith/gospel-fare/bridle-your-empathy-so-that-you-can-truly-love/.

Falconer, Robert. The Others Within Us. Great Mystery Press, 2023. https://robertfalconer.us/the-others/.

Festinger, L., H.W. Riecken, and S. Schachter. When Prophecy Fails. Pinter & Martin, 2008. https://books.google.com/books?id=EsEVBAAAQBAJ.

Fitzpatrick, S., and R. Gellately. Accusatory Practices: Denunciation in Modern European History, 1789-1989. University of Chicago Press, 1997. https://books.google.com/books?id=hLKAQgAACAAJ.

Fromm, Erich. "Marx's Concept of Man." Accessed June 11, 2024. https://www.marxists.org/archive/fromm/works/1961/man/ch06.htm.

Works Cited

Fukuyama, F. Identity: The Demand for Dignity and the Politics of Resentment. Farrar, Straus and Giroux, 2018. https://books.google.com/books?id=OjpIDwAAQBAJ.

Full Speech of Giorgia Meloni at WCF Verona 2019, 2022. https://www.youtube.com/watch?v=0wqovctNVrg.

Furious Mother Slams Her Children's School Board for Enforcing Critical Race Theory, 2021. https://www.youtube.com/watch?v=WRK9NEZGnTw.

Gajdics, Peter. "Gay Not Queer." Quillette, November 25, 2022. https://quillette.com/2022/11/25/gay-not-queer/.

Godwin, William. Enquiry Concerning Political Justice. Accessed June 11, 2024. https://theanarchistlibrary.org/library/godwin-political-justice.

Goldberg, Jonah. Liberal Fascism: The Secret History of the Left from Mussolini to the Politics of Meaning. Penguin Books Limited, 2009. https://books.google.com/books?id=q_c92MdQDCoC.

Goodman, J. David. "A Year After 'Defund,' Police Departments Get Their Money Back." The New York Times, October 10, 2021, sec. U.S. https://www.nytimes.com/2021/10/10/us/dallas-police-defund.html.

Gramsci, Antonio. "The Revolution Against Capital." Accessed June 11, 2024. https://www.marxists.org/archive/gramsci/1917/12/revolution-against-capital.htm.

Greer, John Michael. "Immanentizing the Eschaton." resilience, January 17, 2007. https://www.resilience.org/stories/2007-01-17/immanentizing-eschaton/.

Grim, Ryan. "How Meltdowns Brought Progressive Groups to a Standstill." Accessed June 11, 2024. https://theintercept.com/2022/06/13/progressive-organizing-infighting-callout-culture/.

Grudin, Theodore. "How White Supremacy Caused the Climate Crisis." Accessed June 11, 2024. https://www.earthisland.org/journal/index.php/articles/entry/how-white-supremacy-caused-the-climate-crisis/.

Haidt, J. The Righteous Mind: Why Good People Are Divided by Politics and Religion. Knopf Doubleday Publishing Group, 2013. https://books.google.com/books?id=U21BxGfm3RUC.

Halperin, D.M. Saint Foucault: Towards a Gay Hagiography. Gay Studies, Literature. OUP USA, 1995. https://books.google.com/books?id=o9ct-YPs66UC.

Harrington, M. Feminism against Progress. Skyhorse Publishing, 2023. https://books.google.com/books?id=pL6nEAAAQBAJ.

Harris, Cheryl I. "Whiteness as Property." Harvard Law Review 106, no. 8 (1993): 1707–91. https://doi.org/10.2307/1341787.

Herzog, Katie. "Ana Kasparian Gets Mugged By Reality." Accessed June 11, 2024. https://www.blockedandreported.org/p/episode-213-ana-kasparian-gets-mugged.

Himel, Jeffrey. "Khmer Rouge Irrigation Development in Cambodia," n.d. http://www.genocide-watch.com/images/Cambodia_11_Apr_07_Khmer_Rouge_Irrigation_Development_in_Cambodia.pdf.

Horkheimer, M. Critical Theory: Selected Essays. Critical Theory Series. Bloomsbury Academic, 1972. https://books.google.com/books?id=YiXUAwAAQBAJ.

I'm A Lesbian Woman & I'm Leaving The INSANE "Progressive" Left, 2020. https://www.youtube.com/watch?v=mzYHBPTfXCI.

Kamau-Mitchell, Caroline. "On Erich Fromm: Why He Left the Frankfurt School." In Revisiting the Frankfurt School: Essays on Culture, Media and Theory, 185–206, 2012.

Works Cited

Kassel, Gabrielle. "Queer Cultural Appropriation: Can Straight Really Be Queer? | Well+Good." Accessed June 11, 2024. https://www.wellandgood.com/queer-cultural-appropriation/.

Kendi, I.X. How to Be an Antiracist. Random House Publishing Group, 2019. https://books.google.com/books?id=6pNbDwAAQBAJ.

Kengor, Paul. The Devil and Karl Marx: Communism's Long March of Death, Deception, and Infiltration. Tan Books, 2020. https://books.google.com/books?id=PtORzQEACAAJ.

Kimball, Roger. "The Perversions of M. Foucault | The New Criterion," March 1, 1993. https://newcriterion.com/article/the-perversions-of-m-foucault/.

Kling, Arnold. "Two Theories of Mind." Econlib. Accessed June 11, 2024. https://www.econlib.org/library/columns/y2021/klingtheoriesofmind.html.

Koenig, Melissa. "50-Year-Old Transgender Woman Shared Pool, Locker Room with Young Girls at Race." Accessed June 11, 2024. https://nypost.com/2023/12/15/news/50-year-old-transgender-woman-shared-pool-locker-room-with-young-girls-at-race/.

Koop, Chacour. "Smithsonian Museum Apologizes for Saying Hard Work, Rational Thought Is 'White Culture.'" Miami Herald, July 17, 2020. https://www.miamiherald.com/news/nation-world/national/article244309587.html.

Lenin, Vladimir. "The Dictatorship Of The Proletariat." Accessed June 11, 2024. https://www.marxists.org/archive/lenin/works/1919/sep/x02.htm.

Londoño, Ernesto "How 'Defund the Police' Failed." Accessed June 11, 2024. https://www.nytimes.com/2023/06/16/us/defund-police-minneapolis.html.

Marchese, David. "Bono Is Still Trying to Figure Out U2 and Himself." The New York Times, October 24, 2022, sec. Magazine. https://www.nytimes.com/interactive/2022/10/24/magazine/bono-interview.html.

Marcuse, Herbert. "Repressive Tolerance." Accessed June 11, 2024. https://www.marcuse.org/herbert/publications/1960s/1965-repressive-tolerance-fulltext.html.

Marilyn Manson Explains Satanism, Aleister Crowley, Anton LaVey, 2017. https://www.youtube.com/watch?v=fAC9RK2k19A.

Marx, Karl. "18th Brumaire of Louis Bonaparte. Karl Marx 1852." Accessed June 11, 2024. https://www.marxists.org/archive/marx/works/1852/18th-brumaire/ch01.htm.

Marx, Karl. "A Contribution to the Critique of Hegel's Philosophy of Right 1844." Accessed June 11, 2024. https://www.marxists.org/archive/marx/works/1843/critique-hpr/intro.htm.

Marx, Karl. "Economic Manuscripts: Capital Vol. I - Chapter One." Accessed June 11, 2024. https://www.marxists.org/archive/marx/works/1867-c1/ch01.htm.

Marx, Karl. "Human Pride." Accessed June 11, 2024. https://www.marxists.org/archive/marx/works/1837-pre/verse/verse20.htm.

Marx, Karl. "Invocation of One in Despair." Accessed June 11, 2024. https://www.marxists.org/archive/marx/works/1837-pre/verse/verse11.htm.

Marx, Karl. "Manifesto of the Communist Party." Accessed June 11, 2024. https://www.marxists.org/archive/marx/works/1848/communist-manifesto/index.htm.

Marx, Karl. "The Pale Maiden." Accessed June 11, 2024. https://www.marxists.org/archive/marx/works/1837-pre/verse/verse24.htm.

Works Cited

Marx, Karl, and Friedrich Engels. "Karl Marx and Friedrich Engels Collected Works, Vol 1." Lawrence Wishart. Accessed June 11, 2024. https://lwbooks.co.uk/marx-engels-collected-works/read-and-search-online.

MathNerd, Holly. "Statement from Fred Sargeant." Substack newsletter. Holly's Substack (blog), October 1, 2022. https://hollymathnerd.substack.com/p/statement-from-fred-sargeant.

Max Horkheimer on Critical Theory, 2011. https://www.youtube.com/watch?v=OBaY09Qi-w0.

McLellan, D. Marxism After Marx: An Introduction. Houghton Mifflin, 1981. https://books.google.com/books?id=fN4PAQAAMAAJ.

Melugin, R.F., and M.A. Sweeney. New Visions of Isaiah. The Library of Hebrew Bible/Old Testament Studies. Bloomsbury Publishing, 1997. https://books.google.com/books?id=wA_odaujfPMC.

Miller, J. The Passion of Michel Foucault. Harvard University Press, 2000. https://books.google.com/books?id=BODdpZCvvrQC.

Monroe-Kane, Charles. "The Not-So-Subtle Subversiveness Of Satan Worship." WPR, October 26, 2019. https://www.wpr.org/religion/not-so-subtle-subversiveness-satan-worship.

Nietzsche, Friedrich. "Beyond Good and Evil." gutenberg.org. Accessed June 11, 2024. https://www.gutenberg.org/files/4363/4363-h/4363-h.htm.

NPR. "Understanding Multiracial Whiteness And Trump Supporters." January 24, 2021, sec. Race. https://www.npr.org/2021/01/24/960060957/understanding-multiracial-whiteness-and-trump-supporters.

Oaks, Dallin H. "Criticism." Salt Lake Tabernacle, May 4, 1986. https://www.churchofjesuschrist.org/study/ensign/1987/02/criticism?lang=eng.

Oaks, Dallin H. "Stand as Witnesses of God." Accessed June 11, 2024. https://www.churchofjesuschrist.org/study/eng/ensign/2015/03/stand-as-witnesses-of-god.

Owolade, Tomiwa. "Antiracism Won't Save You: Robin DiAngelo's New Book Is Self-Help for Narcissistic White People." Accessed June 11, 2024. https://unherd.com/2021/06/antiracism-wont-save-you/.

Pankhurst, Em. "The Trojan Unicorn: QT and Paedophilia, Part II. | Dr Em." Uncommon Ground Media, August 10, 2019. https://uncommongroundmedia.com/the-trojan-unicorn-qt-and-paedophilia-part-ii-dr-em/.

Pankhurst, Em. "The Trojan Unicorn: Queer Theory and Paedophilia, Part I. | Dr Em." Uncommon Ground Media, August 10, 2019. https://uncommongroundmedia.com/the-trojan-unicorn-queer-theory-and-paedophilia-part-i-dr-em/.

Payne, Robert. Marx. El Hombre y La Idea. Simon and Schuster, 1968. https://books.google.com/books?id=s2gEAQAAIAAJ.

Peck, M.S. The Road Less Travelled: A New Psychology of Love, Traditional Values and Spiritual Growth. Ebury Publishing, 2012. https://books.google.com/books?id=bRTZwrOni5EC.

"President Nelson Calls upon Latter-Day Saints 'to Lead out in Abandoning Attitudes and Actions of Prejudice' – Church News." Accessed June 11, 2024. https://www.thechurchnews.com/2020/10/4/23217103/general-conference-october-2020-sunday-morning-session-president-nelson-race-prejudice-equality/.

Works Cited

"Rep. Jamaal Bowman Raising Money off the 'White Supremacy' That Killed Tyre Nichols." Accessed June 11, 2024. https://nypost.com/2023/02/06/rep-jamaal-bowman-raising-money-off-the-white-supremacy-that-killed-tyre-nichols/.

Rosen, Zvi. "The Influence of Bruno Bauer on Marx' Concept Of Alienation." Social Theory and Practice 1, no. 2 (1970): 50–68.

Sanmugathasan, N. "Mao Tse-Tung's Contribution to Marxism-Leninism," n.d. https://www.marxists.org/history/erol/sri-lanka/mao.pdf.

Sargeant, Fred. "Mugged at Burlington Pride." Accessed June 11, 2024. https://www.facebook.com/fred.sargeant.1/posts/

Schimel, L., and R. Labonté. First Person Queer: Who We Are (so Far). Arsenal Pulp Press, 2007. https://books.google.com/books?id=wgQVAQAAIAAJ.

"Seek First the Kingdom of God – Deseret News." Accessed June 11, 2024. https://www.deseret.com/2000/3/4/20776378/seek-first-the-kingdom-of-god/.

Shellenberger, M. San Fransicko: Why Progressives Ruin Cities. HarperCollins, 2021. https://books.google.com/books?id=2lsTEAAAQBAJ.

Solzhenitsyn, Aleksandr. "Acceptance Address by Mr. Aleksandr Solzhenitsyn." Templeton Prize. Accessed June 11, 2024. https://www.templetonprize.org/laureate-sub/solzhenitsyn-acceptance-speech/.

Solzhenitsyn, Aleksandr. The Gulag Archipelago Volume 2. Harper Perennial Modern Classics, 2007.

Staff, POLITICO. "Text of Obama's Fatherhood Speech." POLITICO, June 15, 2008. https://www.politico.com/story/2008/06/text-of-obamas-fatherhood-speech-011094.

The Church of Jesus Christ of Latter-day Saints. "The Family Proclamation." Accessed June 11, 2024. https://www.churchofjesuschrist.org/study/eng/scriptures/the-family-a-proclamation-to-the-world/the-family-a-proclamation-to-the-world.

"The Combahee River Collective Statement." The Combahee River Collective, November 16, 2012. https://www.blackpast.org/african-american-history/combahee-river-collective-statement-1977/.

Tse-Tung, Mao. "ON PRACTICE." Accessed June 11, 2024. https://www.marxists.org/reference/archive/mao/selected-works/volume-1/mswv1_16.htm.

Tumblr, "Twelveclara on Glee," https://www.tumblr.com/islandoforder/166379634289/u-know-whats-wrong-with-tumblr-now-too-many

USC Shoah Foundation. "Cambodian Genocide." Accessed June 11, 2024. https://sfi.usc.edu/collections/cambodian-genocide.

Varela, Nicolas. "David Riazanov, a Revolutionary Scholar of Marxism." Accessed June 11, 2024. https://jacobin.com/2024/02/david-ryazanov-revolutionary-marxism-scholar.

Weikart, Richard. "Marx, Engels, and the Abolition of the Family." History of European Ideas 18, no. 5 (1994): 657–72.

"Why I Don't Need Heavenly Mother." Sunstone Podcast. Accessed June 12, 2024. https://sunstone.org/why-i-don-t-need-heavenly-mother/.

Women's Sports Policy Working Group. "578+ Male* Victories in Female Sports." Accessed June 11, 2024. https://womenssportspolicy.org/253-male-victories-in-female-sports/.

Yancy, Desmon. "Why so Many Black Chicagoans Are Frustrated by the Migrant Crisis - Chicago Sun-Times." Accessed June 11, 2024. https://chicago.suntimes.

Works Cited

com/other-views/2024/05/20/black-chicagoans-migrant-crisis-frustration-racism-disinvestment-alderman-desmon-yancy-south-shore.

Young, Brigham, and John A. Widstoe. Discourses of Brigham Young. Kindle. Deseret Book, 2009.

Made in United States
Troutdale, OR
11/24/2024

25236520R00108